ELEVATE
YOUR
RESULTS

ELEVATE YOUR RESULTS

THE MOST INSPIRING WAY TO TAKE YOUR RESULTS TO THE NEXT LEVEL

Foreword by Dr John Demartini
Human Behaviour Specialist, Educator & Teacher From 'The Secret'

Disclaimer

All the information, techniques, skills and concepts contained within this publication are of the nature of general comment only and are not in any way recommended as individual advice. The intent is to offer a variety of information to provide a wider range of choices now and in the future, recognising that we all have widely diverse circumstances and viewpoints.

Should any reader choose to make use of the information contained herein, this is their decision, and the contributors (and their companies), authors and publishers do not assume any responsibilities whatsoever under any condition or circumstances. It is recommended that the reader obtain their own independent advice.

First Edition 2021

Copyright © 2021 by Author Express

All rights reserved. No part of this publication may be reproduced, stored in a retrieval system, or transmitted in any form or by any means, electronic, mechanical, photocopying, recording or otherwise, without the prior written permission from the publisher.

A catalogue record for this book is available from the National Library of Australia

Creator: Harvey, Benjamin J., author.
Other Authors:
Chan, Michelle | Dowsett, Ben | Kan, Min | Novosel, Tracy | Parry, Dave | Pile, Amanda | Rettie, Angela | Shefket, Sharee | Tindall, Chele | Townsend, Kim | Winzer, Markus O.

Title: Elevate your Results / Benjamin J Harvey.

ISBN: 9781925471595 (paperback)

Published by Author Express
www.AuthorExpress.com
publish@authorexpress.com

Dedication

To fellow learners wanting to take their results to the next level. This book is dedicated to you.

Benjamin J Harvey and co-authors

Foreword by Dr John Demartini

As I travel the world delivering my seminars and workshops, I often meet people who are unfulfilled or dissatisfied with portions of their lives.

One of the main reasons people don't achieve or receive their desired results in life, is that they're not consistently acting or living congruently and in accordance with their true highest values or priorities. They are attempting to live by lower ones on their list of values, which they have assumed to be more important that they actually are.

Like for every human being - you live by a set of evolving priorities or values, from those most important to those least important. Your highest values are those you're spontaneously inspired to fulfill from within. As you move down your list, you require outside motivation to take action. When you set a goal that's aligned with your highest values, you will experience increased confidence, achievement and momentum, and will therefore produce greater and more lasting and fulfilling results.

People who are higher achievers spend more of their time doing what's of highest priority and delegating their lowest priority items. This is the secret to achieving greater results in your life.

Getting clear about what's really important to you and what you would truly love to fulfill or achieve is crucial for outstanding results. A qualified coach or mentor working with or alongside you to ascertain your highest values and to assist you in achieving your desired goals is wise and most efficient. Then you can more effectively structure your life and take more higher priority and inspired actions. When you do, you won't beat yourself up about how you're having trouble attaining your goals – because they are truly your most meaningful objectives. Realise that all of us, in our highest values, are more spontaneous achievers. So make sure you set goals that are spontaneously inspiring and deeply meaningful to you.

What you believe about and say to yourself will have a tremendous impact on your results and what kind of life you'll lead. You are the creator of your own destiny. You write the script of your life with every thought and feeling. The greater your self-worth and the more love and appreciation you have for yourself, the more prosperity, fulfillment and achievement you will bring about.

The secret to great achievement is shifting your mindset from "what can I get" to "what can I also give or contribute?" When you help enough people get what they would love in life, you truly make a difference. And if you're grateful for being able to serve, then you, too, will get what you would love in life.

In my experience, doing what you love and loving what you do in a way that others are served and fulfilled too is the most powerful way to *Elevate your Results*.

Dr John F. Demartini
Human Behaviour Specialist
www.DrDemartini.com

BONUS GIFT

The Elevate YOU
7 Day Transformation

Want to take the top 7 areas of your life to the next level?

There is ONE powerful 'Elevate Process' you can use immediately to improve Your Relationships, Health, Finances, Mindset and any other area of your life.

In this transformational 7 day online course, Benjamin J Harvey guides you through the 'Elevate Process' and how you can improve your life from the inside-out.

Normally valued at $295
Get FREE and instant access here:

www.elevatebooks.com/you

Life Rewards Action. Get started today!

Contents

Results Matter — 1
Benjamin J Harvey

Results from the Heart — 41
Sharee Shefket

The Results Within — 59
Tracy Novosel

Rock-Solid Results — 77
Ben Dowsett

The Write Results — 99
Amanda Pile

Weight Loss Results — 121
Min Kan

Stressless Results — 143
Kim Townsend

Fast-Track your Finances — 167
Dave Parry

Fulfilling Decisions — 193
Angela Rettie

Empowered Results — 211
Chele Tindall

The Inner Path to Success — 231
Michelle Chan

Leading through Being — 247
Markus O. Winzer

"Giving yourself permission
to do what you love is the key to
elevating all areas of your life."

~ Benjamin J Harvey

Benjamin J Harvey
Results Matter

For over a decade, Benjamin J Harvey has studied the psychology of empowerment to help people find the answer to life's most intriguing questions.

Knowing that books like the Elevate series empowers individuals to bring their dreams into reality, Benjamin has assisted thousands of people across the globe to invest in themselves by showing how they can live their dream.

In 2009, he founded Authentic Education with business partner Cham Tang, to help empower people to live abundantly on purpose. As a result, Authentic Education went on to achieve something that has never been done before in the history of personal development. They received the BRW Fast Starters Award in 2013 and then backed it up in 2015 by being named in the BRW Fast 100 as the thirty-eighth fastest-growing company in Australia.

Having delivered well over 10,000 one-on-one coaching sessions, and training thousands of people across the globe, Ben now specializes in guiding people in how they can make a difference by achieving success doing what they love.

Ben has been featured on The Today Show in the Sydney Morning Herald and on ABC Radio.

Benjamin J Harvey

Results Matter

What is mindset and how does it affect your results?

Mindset is defined as an attitude, disposition or mood, but I think it comes down to a set of rules you create to either live the life of your dreams...or not. These rules determine the choices you make, and those choices form your results. If you want to change your results, you first must change the rules you live by.

Your mindset is the very thing that shapes your world through beliefs, assumptions and philosophy of life. It can stop or empower you, so examining all aspects of it is crucial to experiencing the life you want to live.

Mindset is critical in acquiring a loving relationship, having the body you want, enjoying fulfilling holidays, having financial freedom and bringing success into your life, but the unfortunate fact is that it's underappreciated and underutilised.

One of my passions in life is to help people live the life that they love, experience the fulfillment they desire and to spend even more time with their loved ones. This all becomes possible with mindset and action. In every program Authentic Education creates, mindset and understanding how neurons factor into it, is a huge component.

Your education starts with our Turning Point Intensive free event we offer to give back to the community, where the core theme is simply, "Life Rewards Action".

Is it possible to change someone's mindset?

Yes, absolutely, as long as the person is open to change, is willing to look at situations differently and is ready to do whatever it takes to alter their life.

It isn't hard to change someone's mindset. A really good advertisement that shows a different way of looking at a situation can cause a small mindset change. This is why it's important to use caution with what you put into your mind. You're being influenced all of the time by everything around you, both covertly and overtly, and it's time you had a good hard look at what you're infusing into your mind, as it's producing the results you achieve and receive in life.

What do you think stops people from creating change in their life?

I've been helping people create strategies and transformation in their life for ten years with both my coaching business and Authentic Education's PHD programs, and over that time I've discovered there are three core issues people come up against when they want to create some change in their life.

1. **Not taking the time to automate their results.**

   The best of the best have a system for automating their results, but people rarely take time out of their life to work on it. You may have heard the saying, "You need to work *on* your business, not *in* your business." The same goes for life. But after thousands of hours of working with people, I can attest they continue to do tasks that could easily be automated. This means they're still doing a lot of unnecessary heavy lifting.

   People might crave a greater level of self-love, but the fact is, if they don't have time to do what they love, how could they ever expect it to occur? They're burning through their time, so by the end of the week, they have none left to do what they love, and then they wonder why they don't truly love themselves. It's a chicken and egg thing.

2. **An unwillingness to learn how to become their own best coach.**

    There are systems that can help with mindset and emotional issues, such as anxiety and depression, that will create a healthy mind-body connection, so you can have a more fulfilling life.

    However, nobody is taught these systems at any point in time, so they have to go and educate themselves outside the general education system. But people aren't willing to learn how to be their own best healer, and as a result they spend decades battling with issues inside of their mind and body, dealing with emotional traumas and significant events they don't know what to do with years later. They don't realise that if they'd just taken a couple of days out to learn how to self-heal, they'd be able to fix these issues.

3. **Not taking the time to learn the way of the wealthy.**

    A person can spend tons of time and money fixing their mindset, relationships, health, career, connection with family and fitness, but if they neglect one specific area, it can unravel everything else. Some may think it's self-love, or emotions, or worthiness, but it's none of these.

    That area is...wealth. Now unfortunately, a lot of people walk around saying, "Money's not important. It doesn't matter. It doesn't have any relevance." But if you trace back the origins of wealth back thousands of years, you'll discover that whoever was the wealthiest was also the healthiest.

    Most people become stressed out and have arguments about money with loved ones, so it creates stress. And most studies regarding stress, state that it's the origin of almost every major catastrophic disease in the body. Therefore, it's safe to say that money does impact your health, because of the stress it creates.

So you can fix up your relationship until it's the best ever, but if you're flat broke, been kicked out of your home and have to sleep on the street with your partner, that relationship isn't going to survive.

Or let's just say you get your career sorted, but you can't afford to ever go on holidays, because you don't make enough, even though you're always working. You also have no time to devote to relationships or family, which creates huge amounts of stress.

When your self-worth goes up, your net worth goes up in correlation. You need to take the time to learn the way of the wealthy. In doing so, you'll allow all of the other areas to be sustained, because although money doesn't make you happy, it does provide options, and those options can bring happiness.

What role do neurons play in brain function?

Basically, a neuron is a thinking cell. They're designed to last a lifetime in the majority of the brain, and it was originally thought that if you killed one off, you didn't get it back.

But neurons have recently been proven to regenerate in certain areas of the brain by a process called *Neurogenesis*. Little is known about this phenomenon, and research is still being conducted.

These neurons, or thinking cells, are inside of your mind and body, and they allow you to compute ideas and information. If you want to pick up a pencil, the message would have to travel down a whole bunch of neurons and activate all different regions of your mind and body for you to pick it up. A child starts out incapable of getting a cup of water to their mouth, but over time, the precision gets clearer and clearer, until they can get the cup to the exact tilt angle with precision.

That precision is thanks to neurons wiring together and learning how to get the signals to happen at an exact moment in time. The more precision you have with the firing of neurons, the more accurate your behaviours become. It just takes a little time.

Inside of your neurons is this pure light, transmitting in the form of an electrical impulse. Now, if you have a hundred-billion neurons, keep in mind that each one can connect with as many as 10,000 other neurons, which means each one can go in 10,000 different directions. And there are as many as one-thousand-trillion synaptic connections.

So if you think you can't learn something new, think again, because you have one-thousand-trillion different connections, which is just shy of the number of grains of sand on planet Earth.

This means people are chemical and electrical in nature. The computer inside your head is quite powerful. To put things in perspective, nineteen-million volumes of encyclopaedias only adds up to 10,000 terabytes, and you have anywhere from a ten to one-hundred terabyte memory. So while your memory may not be infinite, you will never be able to fill it, because the human memory fades and rewrites itself over time.

But what does this have to do with creating a turning point? The good news is that a neuron rewires itself in about two seconds, so you can change your life that quickly.

But here's the bad news: you can also change it back in two seconds. You've heard the saying that old habits are hard to break? Change is easy. Changing back is just as easy.

So how can someone use this knowledge to produce results in their life?

Even though neurons have received a lot of publicity and are quite famous in the neuroscience world, they're not really what you want to research. In fact, it's not even that interesting anymore. But unfortunately, when neurons were discovered, the scientific world pushed aside some major research they were working on and jumped on the neurons.

This means we're decades, if not centuries, behind what we should have been researching.

In the sixteenth century, Andreas Vesalius discovered white matter. Until then, people believed the brain was only made up of grey matter.

But it wasn't until 1854 that Rudolf Virchow, a German pathologist, physician, scientist, pre-historian and author, decided to identify this white matter for the first time ever. He named it after the Greek word *milos*, which stands for marrow, and created the word *myosin*, or what's now referred to as myelin.

Once advancements were achieved regarding neurons, people blankly decided myelin was just this thing that insulated the neurons, and they stopped researching it, which is unfortunate, because myelin matters more than anything else. It's what produces actual results.

Most neurons consist of three distinct regions: the cell body (or soma), with branching dendrites (receivers) and the axon (which transmits information away from the cell body).

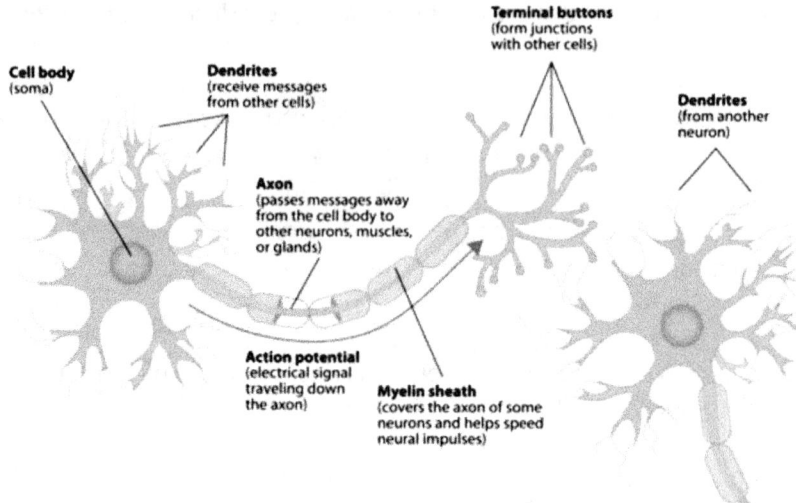

In the science world, the study of myelin was pushed aside, because they believed it was excreted out of the axon, or, in essence, that it wraps and insulates itself. But in 1954, it was discovered that myelin isn't excreted out of the axon. It's actually wrapped onto the axon by glial cells, which in regards to the peripheral nervous system is called a Schwann cell.

All axons in the peripheral nervous system are surrounded by Schwann cells, and the cover produced by these cells is often referred to as the sheath of Schwann.

Schwann cells that surround large diameter axons undergo a wrapping process called myelination. It begins when one part of the Schwann cell moves along the surface of the axon, and the leading edge slides underneath the outer portion of the Schwann cell, pushing it out of the way.

Once the myelination process completes, the cell is myelinated, which means the Schwann cell has covered the axon with many layers of plasma membranes consisting of eighty percent lipids and twenty percent protein, known as the myelin sheath.

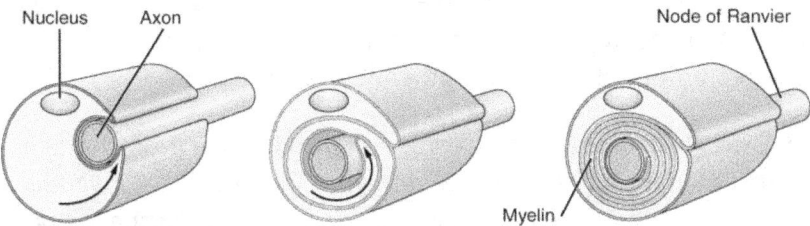

A neuron typically has one axon that connects it with other neurons, or with muscle or gland cells. Some axons can reach from the spinal cord down to a toe. The myelin sheath increases the speed of impulse transmission because the nerve impulse jumps from node to node. The reason this process is important is because the sheath not only insulates the cell, but it allows for precision of activity to occur at a single point.

In 1977, the first-ever magnetic resonance imaging scan was created with an MRI machine, which meant being able to view head traumas noninvasively. This was a major advancement in technology.

In 1985, the diffusion weighted image (DWI), was developed. This is where the MRI machine works out how to observe the diffusion of liquid inside the image.

In 1996 there came the diffusion tensor image (DTI), and for the first time in history, observation of myelin growing around a neuron became possible.

Now, how does this help with rewiring your brain? Well, the more you attempt a new task or way of thinking, the more you keep wrapping myelin around the axon, which means the information can travel faster down that neuron.

In terms of the speed difference, if you can get an axon wrapped proportionately to the diameter of the axon, that axon will travel a hundred times faster than any other neuron in your head.

The way this correlates to having a great life, sitting on the beach making money and hanging out with your friends, is that if you have your axons myelinating correctly, you will get to the destination point of your thinking, actions and behaviours a hundred times faster than the person next to you.

Let me give you a more practical example. If you were playing tennis against a professional and hit a ball to them, by the time they've worked out how they're going to whack it back, it would have taken you a hundred times longer to work it out. In essence, they have the shot ready to go a hundred times quicker than you do. So if it takes them one second to line up their shot, it would take you over a minute and a half before you were even close to being ready.

To myelinate a new road effectively, practise one action over and over again until it becomes unconscious competence. If you wanted to myelinate the perfect tennis serve, you would practice drawing the tennis racket back over and over, until you had the perfect angle. Just that one action, over and over again. If you make an error, stop, reset and start again. Then once you have the serve perfected, you move on to the next step, which would be throwing the ball up in the air over and over, until it produces the exact same result. You go through this for each piece in the serve, until they're perfected, and then you put it all together. This practical step-by-step action myelinates the roads to the perfect tennis serve. It's as simple as that. But people aren't taught this way.

When you myelinate the roads you want, you end up at your destination much faster, which means the actions you take are a hundred times faster with a hundred times more precision, and you get to where you want in life a lot quicker.

How does this relate to forming new habits?

What I'm getting across to you is the concept that at the end of the day, it's not about the neurons, it's about how you insulate them that's important. The more you're able to insulate the ones you want, the easier it becomes.

Many people in my industry believe that if you change your neurons, you change your wiring, and your traumas vanish. But myelin wraps, it doesn't unwrap, unless you're in the 0.000001% of the human race who has a major degenerative neurological illness. This means behaviours related to traumas you experienced when you were a kid still exist inside your mind. Now while you may think this is bad news, it isn't, because if it doesn't unwrap, then all you have to do is wrap the ones you want and stop wrapping the ones you don't.

It's unfortunate that a lot of therapy out there gets you to continually wrap the roads that don't need further insulation. You can get wisdom from your past, but every time you go back to it, just know you're wrapping myelin around it. In the last five years, there have been advancements in transformational technologies where the therapist no longer asks, "Would you please tell me the origin of your experience?" This is because of the research surrounding myelin.

I do a lot of therapy where I go back and check my past to gain an understanding of the origins of my current situation, but I'm aware of exactly what I'm doing.

You speak to anybody who used to smoke and ask them, "How quickly could you light up a cigarette if you really wanted to?" "In the blink of an eye" is usually the answer, but because they've formed the new identity of "I'm not a smoker anymore", they don't. However, the roads where the smoking exists are going to be wrapped for the rest of their life.

People in the personal development industry don't want to tell you this, but I will, because if you know the truth, then you can work on getting past it.

There's a saying that goes, "It's not that we know so much, it's that we know so much that isn't so."

Warren Buffett said, "The chains of habit are so light, you can't feel them until they're so heavy you can't break them."

If you keep myelinating the stuff you don't want, the road gets easier to travel, but if you start myelinating the roads you do want to take, your life changes. Again, you can myelinate a new road in less than two seconds.

Myelin doesn't discriminate. All it responds to is what you ask it to wrap. And it knows this through urgent repetition. That's it. Anything you do urgently and repetitively, it wraps, and vice-versa.

Let's say you're going to Santorini and will spend a couple of weeks there.

During your trip, you're picking up the language. "Wow!" you say. "Look at me speaking Greek". But then five months later you try to remember what you learned, and all you have left are maybe a couple of words or phrases. That's it. This is because when you were in Greece, you were firing those neurons repetitively, which means you were myelinating them. Then when you got back, there was no longer a reason to go down those roads, so you just left them where they were, to the point you can barely even find them. They're still present, you just don't know where you put them.

For instance, you probably can't remember what you had for lunch last Tuesday. Do you know why? Because you didn't myelinate it. Finding a fifteen-year-old memory of a major event is easier, because thanks to the media, you've wrapped it again and again, so when you fire the idea, you find the thought.

How can people use myelinating to change their life?

If you want to change your life starting today, just myelinate what you want. That's it. This is why this chapter is named *results matter*, because anything you wrap in myelin gets you the results you want.

When people talk about manifesting, they're talking about myelin and the production of it. Now, the good news is that you can speed up and slow down the production of myelin.

There's a way to increase myelin by a thousand times faster than the person sitting next to you, so it will look to the naked eye like you're performing miracles. Again, it doesn't discriminate. It takes the pressure off, but it also gets rid of all your excuses.

What is the Triune Brain?

Back in 1960, a neuroscientist and physician named Paul D. MacLean put forth the idea of the Triune Brain complex. He hypothesized that your brain existed in three evolutionary phases.

1. **The R-complex or reptilian brain**

    MacLean said that humans have a brain in common with reptiles.

    The R-complex is what's referred to quite often as the hindbrain or the brainstem. So the reptilian brain does survival instinctual behaviours, like breathing and other bodily functions, as well as ritual and territorial style activities.

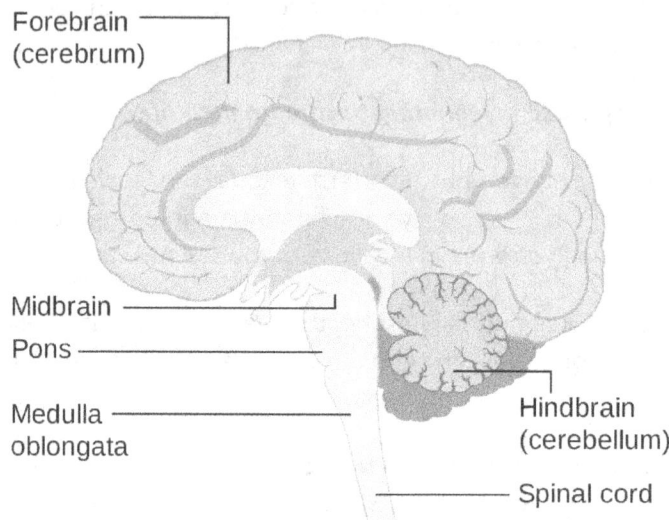

2. **The Paleomammalian complex**

   From the R-complex you evolve into the Paleomammalian complex, which is from the Palaeolithic times. This is where you start to develop a conscious connective idea regarding reward centres and the ability to feel emotion and understand social cues.

3. **Neomammalian complex**

   The Neomammalian complex is the latest addition and the most advanced piece of software, but it's actually the slowest technology you have in your brain.

   It's responsible for language, planning, prioritisation, discernment, willpower and your ability to look in a mirror and recognise yourself.

So until this part of your brain was formed, you wouldn't have known who the heck was staring back at you in the mirror or be able to speak to people.

What are the roadblocks in the way of people getting the results they desire?

Say you have a desire in your heart that you want to create something, whether it's a house by the beach or travelling the world or having a loving relationship. To get to your goal, you first have to get past the roadblocks on Myelin Road.

"YES TOWN"

Intelligence — $E = mc^2$ — Logic, planning, discernment and self-awareness

Imagination — Emotions, maps, social meaning, dreams & rewards

Instincts — Survival, breathing, heart rate, territorial & ritual behaviour

▶ **Checkpoint One: Instincts**

This is where your instincts will work out whether or not you're allowed to produce myelin. If your instincts say no, then no myelin will be produced, and you can't get to your goal.

Now, instincts are all about survival, such as heart rate, breathing, territory and ritual behaviour. At this checkpoint you're analysed from an instinctual perspective, and they're checking seven specific filters. Remember, if you don't get through checkpoint one, you don't make any myelin and get a hundred times faster. If someone can get their dream house in one day, it's going to take you a hundred days to get yours.

Here are the seven filters:

- **Filter one: Fear**

    This is where your fear level is gauged regarding your goal. Now, you can create myelin when you have fear. There are a lot of people who experience it and still take action. It's been said that courage is not the absence of fear; it's getting through the fear, because what you want is much more important.

    Removing fear isn't the essential element, but having something more important is, so it's about mitigation.

- **Filter two: Doubt**

    How much doubt is there around what you're about to do? Are you feeling as if it's impossible? That you don't have the skills or stamina to make it happen?

- **Filter three: Danger**

    There's usually a degree of danger in every major life change. Do you feel you can't combat those dangers? Do they seem like too much for you to handle?

- **Filter four: Suspicion**

    Suspicion creates doubt and mistrust. For instance, if you want to travel the world, you might be suspicious of meeting people who have different cultures and beliefs. Or maybe you have a suspicion that someone making a great offer is trying to swindle you.

- **Filter five: Boredom**

    If you think of doing something that bores you, you'll never start it. You can't myelinate it. If you get up to checkpoint one and say, "Hey, I want you to myelinate the most boring thing ever," it won't get insulated. The same goes for fear, doubt and danger. Your instincts won't allow you to myelinate any of these, because your instincts are saying, "Don't get better at boredom…Don't get better at fear…Don't get better at danger."

- **Filter six: Uncertainty**

    Your instincts don't want you to get better at uncertainty, because the more uncertainty you have in your life, the less-likely your reptilian brain can protect you from imminent danger.

    Your hindbrain loves repetition. It doesn't know what's good or bad. It just knows what didn't kill you. If yesterday you smoked twenty-five cigarettes and you didn't die, checkpoint one says, "Smoke 'em again, and don't smoke any fewer than that, because if you do, we could die!" This is why people repeat the most ridiculous behaviours that are absolutely detrimental to their long-term life experience. Filling your lungs with tar isn't the best thing for your lungs, but uncertainty isn't going to wrap that.

Checkpoint one only understands right now. This second. At most, a day.

✓ **Filter seven: Complication**

   Anything that's complicated won't be wrapped, because if it keeps wrapping more and more complex things, it won't know how to deal and protect you in a more complicated environment, so it likes to try and keep things as simple as possible.

These are the seven filters reviewed at checkpoint one before it makes the decision to myelinate anything.

Doubt often leads to fearing danger, so check for more than one filter at once, such as any uncertainty you're having about your goals.

If you wanted to write a book, you might doubt if anyone will buy it, which prevents the myelination from occurring. But just because you have these concerns, doesn't mean you can't move through them.

Checkpoint one is all about this concept of where your beliefs are formed. Everyone has beliefs that prevent them from moving forward in life, and a lot of checkpoint one is about them. If truth is that which never changes, then your beliefs can't be your truth, because they're transient.

As you travel around the world, your belief system gets destroyed, because what you absolutely think is the truth, you realise is just a belief. A lot of checkpoint one is your storage of beliefs that aren't real at all but are ones you think are helping you survive. They're not. They're limiting you from experiencing all that life has to offer.

▶ **Checkpoint Two: The realm of imagination**

   This is where you store your emotions, maps, social meaning, dreams and rewards. In order to create myelin, you need to have a pre-existing imagination around what it is you want to create.

   In your imagination, you have these maps around incidents that have shaped the way you view the world. If you leave the house with your imagination filled with exactly what they want, you'll see those opportunities. If not, you won't.

For instance, let's say you want to buy your dream house, but the only pictures in your imagination are of you trudging to a job every day you think is boring and lying in bed all day just tuning out and watching television.

If you get to checkpoint two without one image in your head of living in your dream home, you'll be stopped in your tracks, because this is where they scan for patterns.

The people who go out there and create an incredible level of myelin, achieve the most amazing results. They're the ones who spend hours and hours imagining the life they want. The whole world just becomes a breeze when you can understand myelin, because it doesn't care who you are. It just does its job when you activate it.

You have millions and billions of bits of information that are bombarding you all the time. In order for you to not get totally overwhelmed and have a nervous breakdown, your brain has a filtering process where it chunks that down to seven pieces of information. But when you become aware of one thing, you forget about the next, and so on.

The rule of thumb is seven, plus-or-minus two chunks, because that's how many you can handle at any given time and still feel okay. So from three billion down to seven, plus or minus two chunks, with 132 bits per chunk, which is a small amount of information.

All of these bits of information bombard your sense doors. They go through space, time, matter and energy before being filtered through your values language, memories, decisions and belief systems. Then you filter it through your attitude toward life, until all that's left is a small amount of information that lands on the screen of your mind's eye, which becomes your reality.

If you perceive that the whole world is filled with opportunity, then no matter what enters your senses, you'll filter it into the golden cup of opportunity, which affects your emotional state, physiology and behaviour. Then due to this filtering, you project this idea out into the world and see only opportunities everywhere you look. From there you can reach out and grab hold of it, and all of a sudden what you're projecting becomes the way you perceive the world.

Wayne Dyer, who was a mentor of mine, would often say that there are two types of people in the world: those who walk out of the house looking to be offended and those who see opportunity everywhere, and you have to decide which one you are.

Your reality is determined by your imagination and what you filter, which has a huge impact on the way you perceive the world.

> **Checkpoint Three: Intelligence**

This is about perception.

Intelligence is the realm of language, planning, prioritisation, discernment, willpower and self-awareness. It's also where you store different types of value systems.

If you can get yourself through all three checkpoints, you can get that myelin created. The whole idea behind the concept is to have all of them communicating in the same language.

You might feel like there are multiple types of communication going on inside your mind. For instance, you imagine having a beautiful car, but you're scared of someone scratching it, so you drive around in a beat-up clunker. Or every night you imagine having a loving partner, but you're petrified of being rejected, so instead you go to clubs on the weekends, get as drunk as possible, pass out and go home.

There are actually three conversations going on within you: your intelligence, your emotional state and your physiological actions (your mind, body and spirit). As you look more deeply, you'll discover that the secret to getting myelin to produce at the fastest level is to get all three of them to line up as one congruent conversation.

Why do people feel they need to get permission before they make a major change in their life?

Wayne Dyer believed we live in a permission-based reality.

But what does this mean?

When you first arrive on this planet, you're myelinating like crazy, and a lot of that myelination forms your imprint.

Because you've just myelinated stuff so thoroughly, it's almost impossible to break. In fact, psychologists and psychiatrists say that who you are as a person, meaning your personality type, traits, behaviours, distress patterns, and what makes you happy and sad, is set up before the age of five. That's how deep this myelin goes.

So as you go through the process, you're myelinating a lot of permission. May I go to the bathroom? May I stay up late? May I sit down?

What happens is that you myelinate the belief that you need permission from somebody else before you do anything in your own world. For instance, ninety-five percent of your behaviours surrounding money were set up before the age of ten, unless you've reprogrammed it, but very few people do.

Ask yourself who your influences were in regard to money, including your emotional state surrounding it. You'll probably be mortified to discover that the person who holds your bank account is younger than ten years of age, and their investment decisions are based around instant gratification.

I love the simplicity of everything Wayne Dyer taught. He said there were just two little words you needed to say over and over again: *I'm allowed.*

Go ahead and print them out on a sheet of paper and stick it inside your front door, so just before you leave the house you say, "I'm allowed."

Think about that. Wouldn't it be ridiculous to call up a friend to give them permission to do what they love? Of course, because it would be condescending. But believe it or not, people will continue along their path, until someone tells them it's okay to do something else. Of course, that's not going to happen.

However, that little imprinted myelinated section of your brain was fully set up with a permission idea. In fact, until you left home, you still had to get permission to do anything.

When achieving a goal, is it better to go it alone or with a team?

In regard to transformation, there's a Native American proverb that you go faster on your own, but further as a team.

If you follow through on your New Year's resolution and join a gym, the chances of you quitting is well above forty percent, as in not using it and giving up in a matter of three months. But if you join that gym with a friend, even if you don't work out on the same machines or take the same class together, your chance of cancelling your membership goes to less than five percent.

I'm a big fan of empowering your peer group and working out how to get the right people around you, because quite often those you hang around have a huge impact on what you do in life.

Everyone wants to be wealthy, but few people ever add someone who's wealthy to their peer group, and then listen to what they have to say about wealth. Or people who want to be happier don't go out of their way to add someone to their peer group who knows about emotions.

There's a saying that goes, "The safer you feel, the quicker you heal." Those you surround yourself with are there to make sure you have a safe and supportive environment in which to transform. That's why we created authentic.com.au for people all over the world to have access to the right support and peer groups.

How do people turn thoughts into action?

Many people believe imagination is all you need to turn thoughts into action. They saw the movie *The Secret*, so they sit at home just imagining what they want. And when ten years later nothing's changed in their lives, they say, "I followed everything the movie told me to do! I've been sitting on a milk crate in my house, imagining a Ferrari for years, but there's no Ferrari in my driveway!"

Unfortunately, *The Secret* left out a large chunk of the equation, known as action. There's a saying that goes, "If imagination was all it took, then every seven-year-old girl would have a pony." So, there's more to it than just imagination. It's having the right instincts, filters and level of intelligence, and using them in a precise action. If you get these three areas to work in conjunction, you can move mountains.

What is the success equation?

There's a successful entrepreneur named Kazuo Inamori, who's dubbed the Buddhist Billionaire. The reason he got this name is because he's Buddhist, and he built two multi-billion-dollar companies from nothing. He then rescued a third, Japanese Airways, which he also turned back into a multi-billion-dollar organization.

The guy is a deeply compassionate man and a wise soul who decided to analyse what the secret is to life and the key to getting results. When I read about Kazuo, we changed the entire way we work our company.

It's been said that any fool can make something more complicated, but it takes a genius to simplify it. What he figured out was that anyone who wants to have a successful life, only needs to gauge themselves on three metrics, and if they score highly in all three, their success is guaranteed.

▶ **Metric One: Attitude**

Attitude is scored from negative 100 to plus 100. Since it's calculated by multiplication, if you get a negative on attitude, the rest of your score is negative.

The reason he scored it this way is because he worked out that if you have a bad attitude, no matter what you do, you're going to bring the whole team down.

For instance, you take a negative, low-vibrating entity and put it into a roomful of people. If those people don't have what's called energetic integrity, they can bring the energy down through entrainment, or synching with the more dominant vibration.

When you lower your vibration, your thoughts go lower and more depressive, and when you raise your vibration, your thoughts become higher and more elated.

So if you have a bad attitude, your life is going to be miserable.

- **Metric Two: Effort**

    Kazuo understood that you can't put out negative effort, so it has to be scored from zero to 100.

    So, if you decide to go to the gym, but then put in minimal effort, you're not going to get the results you want.

- **Metric Three: Ability**

    If you have a fantastic attitude and put in a great level of effort, the only thing that will let you down is your skill level.

    For example, let's say you go to the gym and put in more effort than anyone you've ever seen, but you never ask the proper way to use the equipment, so you expend a lot of energy with little result.

    Or maybe you want a better relationship, so you make sure you dedicate an hour of your day to your partner, but you spend the entire time yelling at them.

By excelling at the three elements of attitude, effort and ability, anything can happen, because all of them combined equals myelination.

Be responsible for your life. Have a positive attitude, put in the effort and acquire the right skills.

If you want to fix your finances, have a good attitude about money. Stop saying you hate it and it's not important. Then put in the effort, such as doing something every week that will improve your financial outlook.

If you do all of this, in a short period of time, you'll change your situation. There's no trick to it, but there are ways to develop these abilities, skills, efforts and attitudes, far more rapidly.

Reading doesn't change your life. Applying what you read does. There are people who are into what's called *shelf help* and *shelf development*. It's where you stand back and marvel over your shelf full of manuals.

But what you need to be concerned about is self-development, which means opening up the manual again and acting on it. Because if you're not taking any action, nothing is going to occur. The key to results is the application of knowledge.

A lot of people are reading books, thinking they're going to change, but they don't make the time to do the wonderful techniques contained in these books, because they're too busy running to read the next one.

People don't rise to the level of their expectations; they fall to the level of their training. How is it that after a year of having the exact same teacher, do certain students shine, while others don't?

It has to do with whether you have a short or long-term vision.

When you take someone who practices a musical instrument just twenty minutes a day but has a long-term vision, and compare them to someone who practices ninety minutes a day and has a short-term vision, the person who practices just twenty minutes will reach their goal five times faster. And here's something else to think about. If you get two people who practice the same ninety minutes, but one has a short-term vision and one a long term, the person with the long-term vision has a four-hundred percent greater success rate.

Inside every person is an identity; an idea of who they want to become. Maybe it's expressed or maybe it isn't, but that identity, once activated, allows them to achieve goals five times faster than anybody else. This means if it takes a person five years to write a book, you could do it in one.

This is because the myelin wrapping is accelerated when that myelin is directly correlated to your future identity. So when you line up your goals to your values, which are nothing more than the identity of who you want to be, you start to create remarkable changes.

If a child believes they're going to be a pianist for the rest of their life, as in, their identity is, "I am a pianist," when they go to rehearsal, they practice like a pianist. But somebody who says, "I'm playing the piano until the end of the year" will practice just enough to learn what they have to.

The level of attention to the activity is dramatically enhanced when your identity is true to your activity. This is why I say to people, "If you're not doing what you love, whatever you're doing is a total waste of your life."

This is because if you're doing what you love, you're going to get there five times faster, but if you're not, you'll constantly be miserable, because everyone is outperforming you and succeeding way quicker than you are. By doing what you love, you activate all of the success resources of a long-term vision.

Now, I know many people have learned to make "I am" statements, but I'm going to say something that tends to make people angry: it's a waste of time. If you want your identity statements to work, you have to change it to, *I am, because ... (of this action)*. For example, you'd say, "I am an author, because I write books."

It was discovered that the identity statement, when backed up with action, equalled results. Just saying, "I am happy" isn't enough. You have to say, "I am happy, because I hang out at the beach." Otherwise, your brain doesn't know why you're happy.

What does this mean for you? It means you need to start aligning with your vision and live true to your values. Start doing what you love. Stop following anybody else's vision, because if you do you're going to be five times slower than they are, and every day will be disappointing and leave you wondering, *Why haven't I made it yet?* The answer is, because it's not your vision. And if it's not your vision, you won't produce myelin the same way.

How does a person's values relate to their identity?

Your values play a big part in the formation of your identity. In fact, if you speak to people who study psychology, healing or transformative tools of any description, they'll explain that your identity is made up fundamentally of two things: your values, as in what you deem to be important to you, and your beliefs, as in what you believe to be true at any given moment. There are more aspects, like your capabilities, the environment you live in and your behaviours, but essentially who you are as a person consists of your values and beliefs.

When you talk to somebody and try to gauge their identity, what you're really figuring out is their values and beliefs. The stronger your identity, the faster you develop that myelin.

Your whole world is shaped by your values, so when you look at the world, you're filtering predominantly through your value systems. In other words, if your profession is collecting garbage, all you'll see are rubbish bins and how to angle your truck to pick them up. Or if you're a property developer, all you'll see are property opportunities.

To put it in more practical terms, I'd like to discuss joint bank accounts and why I disagree with them.

If a couple both pulls from the same pool of money, and it's only spent in accordance with one person's values, the by-product is called resentment, which then builds up, and all of a sudden you have a breakdown in the relationship. Forty percent of all divorces have to do with disagreements over money.

One person is going to have this thing in the back of their head, just ticking away, which leads to arguments and divorce, all because they couldn't have an open conversation about how to spend the money.

How can people resolve value conflicts and move forward?

Value conflicts can be both internal and external, meaning you can get into arguments with yourself.

Once you know your values, you can start to engineer your life to fulfil them. There are two ways to be successful in life:

1. Change your values to match your goals. (Not recommended)

2. Set your goals to match your values. (Recommended)

Most people set their goals to match other people's values, and they wonder why life is so hard. What I say to them is, "You've got to get on track and then have a crack." What I mean is that you have to get onto your values track, and then have a go. Don't have a go at life if you're not living true to your values.

There's a process to run through that will allow you to get clear about what your values are. It's called the Values Track, in which you identify five core categories that are important to you. Once you identify them, you can start to have a look at your identity.

But first, you need to get the base-level values sorted out and move on from there. If you don't get on track before having a crack at life, you're wasting your time. These are the five core categories:

1. **Talk**

    There are certain subjects you love talking about and ones you hate talking about.

When people talk outside of your values, you don't like them, and when they talk inside of your values, you love them. Given the opportunity, you will direct the conversation to something you enjoy talking about. You can't stop it.

2. **Research**

Would you admit that when no one else is around, you do research? You just get online or open up books. You can research until 3:00 in the morning, and not one person asked you to do it.

3. **Acquire**

You might practice the guitar or singing or writing. These are the skills you acquire, and the reason is because you value and love them.

4. **Contemplate**

There are some things you contemplate more than others. You have to get in touch with what those are and how they make you feel. For instance, you may daydream about travelling, and the feeling you get from it is freedom.

5. **Knowledge**

Inside your mind, you have bucketloads of knowledge. Some of it is completely disorganised, and some of it is really, really organised. If your knowledge is organised, this is a direct indicator that you love it, because you only organise what you love, and you disorganise what you don't.

For example, you may know how to knit, but it's not one of your favourite activities, so each step of the process may come slowly to you, whereas you love making lasagne and do it all the time, so you could quickly rifle off the steps to make it.

Disorganising a relationship is a symptom that you're falling out of love with the person. If you stop organising time and quality conversations together, it's the first indicator that you're falling out of love with them. You disorganise things to move away from them, and you organise what you enjoy.

Inside your mind you have information that's organised and you're proficient at. Whether you admit it or not, it's in there.

So, let's say your values track included healing, spirituality, presenting and travel, but you make a living as an accountant. This means you're off-track. Or even if you own your own business, but it has nothing to do with those values, you're still off-track.

Now if you travel the world speaking about spirituality and healing, you're totally on track.

So the fact is, you may know your values track, but you don't always give yourself permission to live true to it. Just because you know your values, doesn't mean you live them. There are people out there who say your life demonstrates your values, but it's not really true. Your life demonstrates your beliefs until you remove them, and then it demonstrates your values. You could be trapped by your own belief systems.

How does a person's belief system play into their value system?

If every time you try to escape you hit a wall, it means you're stuck in your belief systems. Psychologists call this your boundary conditions.

So if you know your values are spirituality, healing, presenting and travel, but you're an accountant, and someone asks why you don't travel the world sharing spiritual knowledge, your response might be, "Because I'm not smart enough" or, "It won't pay the bills" or maybe, "Well, because my dad was an accountant, and my mum was an accountant, and her mum was an accountant." These are all beliefs.

So your values are trapped inside of your belief systems, and until you shift your beliefs, you'll never live a life true to your values. But the good news is that you can destroy these beliefs, and once you clear them out, your values are then free to express themselves throughout your life.

There are those who refuse to live true to their values track. They say, "Oh, this thing? It won't pay the bills, so I'll just keep doing what I hate." But there are people out there who do what they love, and they still have bills. So if you're never going to be able to get rid of your bills, you may as well just go for it.

My advice is to do your best to get fully on track, but this is hard to do when the beliefs are blocking you, so seek knowledge as to what your values might be.

How does someone achieve a long-term vision?

Let's say you get through all of your filters: Fear, doubt, danger, suspicion, complication, boredom and uncertainty. At this point you have eight specific functions that when you turn them all on, will create miraculous goal achievement. If you see people who just accomplish things as if by magic, and you can't work out how the heck they did it, it's because these eight specific functions in their brain all switched on at once.

To reinforce the concept, I'd like to give you an example of how powerful it is when you're able to accomplish this, which is rare and only happens when you have a good reason for doing it. If you don't, you may only switch on two or three, but rarely all eight. By linking them all together with the highest density of myelin, you'll become a fully functioning human being who can achieve anything.

For instance, let's say I asked you to come up with $15,000 in five hours. You'd probably say it was impossible.

But what if I kidnapped the person you loved most in the world. Would your answer change? This example is used all the time in personal development, but few people ever bother to explain the process to you, so I'd like to do that.

When you had no reason to acquire the money, you didn't turn on the eight essential functions that are required to manifest it out of thin air.

The question is, why did the situation have to get to such extremes before you started to get resourceful? Because something did change in your psychology. Something clicked. And it was these eight functions.

So someone kidnaps a person you love, and all of a sudden you find the money. How did you go from having nothing to having $15,000 on the spot? The answer is that you started becoming resourceful, because you had to stretch your mind to think of every possibility.

Jim Rohn has a famous quote that Tony Robbins picked up and made even more famous: "It's never a matter of resources. It's only a matter of resourcefulness."

The $15,000 was always waiting for you out there, you just needed to be resourceful in the way you acquired it. That resourcefulness can only occur when eight functions in your brain start working. And when they do, you become infinitely resourceful, because you have a strong Why. Straight away you're borrowing money…you're selling your car… you're busking…you're taking a loan.

So here's a situation where you believe you can't afford to pay your rent or go on holidays, but yet if the situation called for it, you'd be able to come up with $15,000 in five hours. This is proof that you're not going to make money in any of your ventures, until you have a strong Why. Your wealth is waiting for you to find it.

This series of eight functions working together is known as the executive function.

Once this happens, you can manifest what you want out of thin air. Though I used the money example, because it's clean and quick, it could be anything, such as emotions, health and relationships. The executive function's job, if you listen carefully, is instantaneous goal achievement.

When you turn on executive function, it goes beyond myelin production and to a whole other threshold of achievement. Each individual component has different functions, but when you get all eight working together and ask, "What is the core function of those eight functions?" the answer is the achievement of goals. That is its sole job description. Not the setting of goals. Not the visualising of goals. Not the strategising of goals. The actual achievement of the goal itself. The completion of the task.

Here are the eight factors that make up executive function:

1. **Impulse control**

    The first thing that happens when you have a meaningful Why is that you immediately get impulse control. This is when you're doing a task, but you get an impulse to maybe check your social media, eat a piece of chocolate cake or stare at the television, but instead of riding the impulse, you choose to stay on task.

    If you don't have a strong Why, then when a strong impulse comes up, instead of controlling it, you act upon it and therefore don't get to where you were headed.

    So, impulse control is the ability to stop and think before acting, which happens when you possess a meaningful Why and have activated executive function.

2. **Organisation**

   When you activate executive function, organisation kicks in. This is the ability to create and maintain systems and keep track of information materials and resources to achieve your goal.

3. **Self-monitoring**

   Self-monitoring is when you're aware of who you are and monitor and evaluate your own performance. Functions of what's classed as the third eye, such as having awareness, doing meditations, scanning yourself and observing who you are as a person, are an executive function. Spiritually, it's called, awareness. So when you have awareness of the self, the body, soul or emotions, it means you've strengthened the executive function of self-monitoring.

4. **Emotional control**

   Emotional control is when you say, "I can manage my feelings by thinking appropriately about my goals." If you can't control your emotions, it has a huge impact on your achievement of goals.

   In fact, Warren Buffet said that if you can't manage your emotions, you shouldn't ever expect to manage your money. So, your emotions have a huge impact on your ability to achieve a goal, but if you keep getting swayed emotionally from side to side, you'll never follow through with it. Many people lose their goal achievement because of their emotional state. One little snafu happens, and they snap. They get annoyed for five weeks, finally get over it, and then another little thing happens, and they snap. Two years later, nothing has changed, because their executive function is broken.

5. **Flexibility**

   If you have flexibility, it means when things don't go your way, you just bend, and move, and flex around the whole idea. You have the ability to change strategies and revise plans when conditions change.

Those who are inflexible are locked into one pathway, and any deviation affects their emotions. They get angry and annoyed. These people can suspend or halt a team project, due to their refusal to bend.

6. **Working memory**

   Working memory is the ability to kick up a memory into your conscious mind and use it to get the task to happen faster. When you go to take off your watch, you bring up the memory of previous times you've taken it off, hold it in your working memory, and follow it.

   If you couldn't access your working memory, everything would slow down. You'd have to start all over again from the beginning, like you'd never done it before, so working memory has to be functioning in order for you to rapidly achieve your goals.

7. **Task initiation**

   Task initiation is having the ability to recognise when it's time to get started on a task without delay. Procrastination is the symptom of an ineffective Why. If you don't have a good reason for doing an activity, the executive function of task initiation won't start. And if task initiation isn't working, all you experience is procrastination. So, it's the symptom of a weakness in your task initiation function.

   If you decide on doing a task but put it off until you've had your coffee, or it can only be done at a certain time, and that time keeps getting pushed up until you keep promising yourself you'll complete it 'tomorrow', it's because of an ineffective executive function.

8. **Planning and prioritisation**

   Planning and prioritisation is the ability to create steps to reach a goal and make decisions as to what to focus on. It's where the brain actively shifts through the highest priorities and recalibrates itself based on the very next thing that needs to happen.

   Now, if you're able to turn on your executive function during an emergency, such as someone kidnapping your loved one and having to find a way to come up with the money, it means you already have it. But if you can't find the money the first time around, it's evidence you're not using your executive function, because in a life-or-death situation, it should become activated.

   When executive function is working correctly, you can't be distracted by anything. If someone were to come to you and ask you to goof off on social media, play a video game or watch TV, you wouldn't even answer them, because you'd be so focused on accomplishing your goal. Once executive function turns on, you can't be distracted or affected emotionally.

   Imagine you're trying to acquire the $15,000, and someone came up to you and said, "You're a loser." Do you honestly think you're going to get upset by that? No way. You don't have time. You're on project. You're on task.

   People who live true to their *Why* are not emotional, because they don't have time to react to other people's opinions. They're too busy completing an important task. Once executive function is switched on, impulses go, tasks get initiated and distractions vanish, because they're on task. That's the power of turning on executive function.

So if you're wondering what's best to myelinate, it's all eight of these functions. There are scientists who say that it breaches back into other different parts of the lobes around your head, but most of it is found in the white and grey matter of the prefrontal region.

Do you believe science and spirituality are intertwined?

The brain is lazy by default. It follows something called the *Tao Te Ching*, which is the path of least resistance, in order to conserve energy.

Today, science and spirituality are getting closer than ever before. I think there are many concepts in spirituality that science hasn't caught up with yet, and who knows if they ever will, but the overlap between the two ideas can now be understood.

In fact, you don't even have to believe in spirituality anymore, because there's so much science that can back up anything that spiritual people say. I like to have a holistic balance. I come from a deeply spiritual background, but I also believe in the science.

For instance, if someone is clairvoyant (clear seeing), it means their imagination conjures up pictures. Being clairaudient (clear hearing) means being able to hear their imagination and pay attention to their mind chatter. Being clairsentient (clear sensing) means picking up on energies, such as walking into a building or meeting someone and instantly feeling comfortable or awkward in their presence. Having claircognizance (clear knowing) is just "knowing" something. For instance, overhearing someone talk about a certain class on a subject and feeling compelled to ask about it. Or maybe feeling the need to rush home due to sensing a loved one is in danger.

But whether you come from the four clairs or from the science, it doesn't really matter. They're all talking about the same thing. Scientists would say you're turning on executive function to the highest level. Mystics would say if you awaken the soul and the third eye, the universe will writhe at your feet in ecstasy as it conspires for your greatness.

What they're talking about is the capacity to master manifest. But no matter which theory you believe, it's the ability to create miracles in your life. It truly is.

So if you can wire the eight executive functions together and consciously strengthen them, you'll become a goal-achieving machine. Anything you want to create in life is yours for the taking, because to try and achieve a goal without one of them would be a challenging experience.

Unless you had a major traumatic head injury, then chances are your executive function is going for it. And even if you did experience trauma, the good news is that you can just myelinate it starting today. You can rewire all of this stuff and wrap it with no problem at all.

I want you to understand this, because once you do, you'll realise you can accomplish anything and change your life.

 To discover more about how Ben can help you *Elevate Your Results*, simply visit www.elevatebooks.com/results

Sharee Shefket
Results from the Heart

Sharee Shefket is a counsellor, hypnotherapist, mindset coach, Psych-K® practitioner, author and entrepreneur.

With over sixteen years of experience working in mental health, she's helped clients change their lives by coaching them to find the source of their obstacles and define their own strategies. The end result is improved relationships, finding their purpose, building a stronger resilience to adversity and developing a better understanding of their self-identity.

Sharee is on a mission to help people reclaim their personal power by recreating who they would like to be. She teaches them to dismantle the layers of self-limiting beliefs and values and set goals for a fulfilling future.

Sharee has also authored a children's book about empowerment and runs workshops, online programs and retreats.

Sharee Shefket

Results from the Heart

What's your biggest life lesson?

The biggest life lesson I have learned is that you never really know anything. We go to school, have life experiences, become a little wiser and think we know it all. Well, I did. Then I realized I had a biased viewpoint. It was a quote from Maya Angelou that made me understand how I'd limited myself to a typically standard education, and it was time for me to step out of my comfort zone. It goes, "I've learned that I still have a lot to learn". I promised myself that I would never stop learning, because life has many lessons to teach, and it doesn't need to stop once you've completed your formal education.

The moment I changed my mindset, I birthed a new version of myself. I now have such a thirst for knowledge, that I try to consume as much content into my day as I can. I see it all as an opportunity to learn about a topic I'm interested in. Life, after all, is one big classroom.

What does love mean to you?

LOVE! The four-letter, elusive word that is the basis of many songs, films and heartbreaks. Love, for me, is more than just a feeling. It's what I am. Sounds a little cliché, I know, but it is. You see, I use love as the core for everything I do now. There's a saying that goes, "Do you think with your brain or heart?" This is what I'm talking about. I shifted to a heart-centred approach to life and started making the right decisions for me. Love is being human.

If you were speaking to your younger self, what advice would you give?

The advice I'd give to my younger self would have to be, "Don't take life too seriously. Allow yourself to have more fun". I teach this to my children all the time.

What would you say is your slogan for life?

I was recently invited to a high school to talk about stress management. My key advice was to not ignore the stress but to use it to their advantage as an energy boost instead. If I had one of those slogan T-Shirts made, it would be, *Take a deep breath, and have a big belly laugh!*

When you catastrophize a future event, like exams for instance, you go into fight/flight/freeze mode and lower your IQ. The prefrontal cortex is the rational, executive-thinking part of your brain, which is useful when undertaking an exam.

Unfortunately, the word "stress" has seeped into our everyday conversation. Reframe the word by changing the meaning behind it. See it as an abundance of energy instead. So, if you keep saying to yourself, *I'm feeling stressed*, change it to *I have an abundance of energy right now*. This will minimise the chance of you sending a message to your amygdala that you're in danger and need to go into survival mode.

When I look back at the younger version of me, I can see that I didn't allow myself to have much fun. I took exams way too seriously and put myself in such a stressful state when I didn't need to.

Sharee Shefket

Have you ever had a wake-up call?

My wake-up call was more like a slap in the face. It's difficult even now to truly comprehend it all.

I had two unusual events. The first incident was an attempted carjacking. What was extraordinary about this was not the attack per se, but the overwhelming feeling that I was in significant danger just before the attempt, which made me lock my car in the nick of time. After the aggressive attempt, I swiftly took a record of the man's number plates. But when I reported the incident to the police, they dismissed it as nothing too sinister.

I went home that day with an awful feeling that his intention was to kill me. I spoke with my husband and some friends about it, and they also thought maybe I was reading too much into it. But the next day, I couldn't shake the feeling that I'd somehow cheated death.

A few days later, I'd put the whole incident behind me, when I received a phone call from a senior detective to come into the station immediately. The man stabbed a woman, and they wanted me to identify him. The police were now curious as to how I was able to lock my car within minutes (actually, more like seconds) of his carjacking attempt. They needed an explanation I couldn't provide for them. At the end, they told me to play the lotto, due to my tremendous luck.

A few months after this event, I went to New Zealand with my family to celebrate the new year. We booked the Sky Hotel in Auckland, as we wanted to be close to the fireworks display. We had a lovely dinner and waited just outside of the hotel for them to begin.

A few minutes before midnight, my husband noticed the big crowds coming along and thought he could quickly drop off his expensive bulky camera in the hotel room before the fireworks show. He didn't make it back in time, so I quickly moved my two young daughters out of the crowd and closer to the entrance of the hotel, so my husband could find us more easily. I had my four-year-old daughter in my arms, so she could see the fireworks better, when suddenly, a man attacked.

At first, I assumed there was some kind of fight, and we accidently got caught up in it. I soon learned this wasn't the case and went into mother protection mode. I covered my youngest daughter's head while trying to grab my other daughter's hand, so we could move out of the way. But before I could make a move, the man held onto my arm and kept punching me in the head repeatedly, until I concussed and fell to the floor.

I woke up in a New Zealand hospital bed. The nurses didn't want me to see my reflection in the mirror, so they covered them up with newspapers. At that moment, I really didn't care about my appearance, I just wanted to know if my kids were okay. The nurse said they were fine. They were conducting tests on my youngest daughter, while my eldest daughter was being looked after by some Japanese tourists who'd helped her find my husband.

Following my recovery, I received a letter from the New Zealand Police to let me know that they were not able to identify the man who'd assaulted me. They later followed up with a phone call, and the officer suggested that I was lucky and unlucky at the same time, and I should buy a lotto ticket. I thought, *Where have I heard that before?*

Was the universe trying to tell me something? I had many questions about why all of this was happening. Was I lucky or unlucky? At that time in my life, I was totally clinical in my work and cynical of all things spiritual. There were some other minor but unexplainable events that followed, which I could no longer ignore. I cherish my life so much more now. This was the start of the spiritual awakening I'd been avoiding all my life.

What is your big WHY?

When the subject comes up of my big Why, I think about this quote by Simon Sinek, that goes, "People don't buy what you do, they buy why you do it. And what you do simply proves what you believe".

So, my big Why is to impact as many people in a positive way as I can, by empowering them. I truly believe that each one of us is a powerful being, but we forgot how to use our superpowers. My mission is to help them ignite their passion again. We're not broken. We've just allowed events, words, beliefs and people to take away our personal power, and I coach my clients to reclaim it again. I love the moment when I see them light up. It also lights me up and brings me so much joy.

What do you think is your life purpose?

According to the Japanese word *ikigai*, your life purpose is the reason you get out of bed.

It took me awhile to figure this one out, but once I did, I began helping others find their purpose. I struggled, because I overcomplicated it. What I mean is that I had this idea that your life purpose had to be monumental. In fact, it's quite simple, and we often think we offer little value if we can't figure it out.

What I discovered was that our life purpose is simply to love, but it's the way you package the love that's different from person to person. I love each of my clients as a fellow human being, regardless of their circumstances or what they've done in their lives. I come in with no judgement, and that's the space I hold for them. This is the love I provide.

Everyone has love they can share with the world. I heard about an elderly Japanese man who owned a humble food stand. His sushi was sought after by people in Japan, and even famous people all over the world. He didn't care for millions of dollars and declined offers to expand his business. He just wanted to keep things simple. Making the sushi and watching people enjoy each morsel of food was his joy...his *ikigai*. He made each piece of sushi with love and offered that to the world.

How are you making a difference in people's lives?

I'm making a difference by empowering them to live the best way they can. I observe too many people wishing their life away, waiting for something external to occur before they give permission to themselves to feel joy. As soon as they get close to their goal, they feel happy for a moment, and then it starts wearing off.

Then they start searching for something else to get that feeling again. This goes on for years, before they get to a certain age and start asking themselves questions like, *Is that all there is?* Despair settles in, and some relationships begin to implode. This is when the client comes to visit me in the clinic. I help them to first clean up any destruction that has occurred. It's like demolishing a house that's no longer serving them. Then we push up our sleeves and work on building a new version of themselves. I love seeing who they become, because it's free from everyone else's expectations and self-limiting beliefs. They break free from their programming of who they thought they were or had to be. It really is a cathartic experience.

What are you passionate about?

I'm passionate about many things, but if I had to choose only one, it would be deep and meaningful connections with others and discussions about the nature of our reality. I'm one of those people who loathes talking about the weather. Small-talk is necessary on occasion, but most people just stop there, and I think it's because they have a fear of intimacy.

The real magic occurs when you start connecting with someone beyond the superficial talk. You find out so much about that other person, which means they also know more about you. There might be family you've known your whole life and think they really know who you are. However, if you've never gone deeper than small talk, then sadly, they really don't know you at all.

What do you think people's biggest problems in life are?

The biggest problems that I witness time and time again is old, redundant programming. According to Dr Bruce Lipton, a child from the time of birth to approximately the age of seven, is predominantly in a theta brainwave, which basically means they're in hypnosis. They're downloading programming from their parents, family, school and society. As they grow older, they continue to reinforce this programming. Most people aren't even aware of it.

For example, a common problem I see is when people say they'd like to change a habit but have difficulty once their motivation wanes. They assume that they don't have enough willpower.

Unfortunately, your subconscious mind doesn't like you changing the program. This gives people the impression they can't change. It's such a misconception, that it disempowers them. As soon as my clients understand how their internal programming works, they start to see themselves differently.

What is the best way to help them with this problem?

Once the programming is acknowledged, it's time to undo it all. I often use an analogy of a computer technician. I work with clients to figure out what programming is no longer serving them and what new beliefs they would like to install. The undoing of all the old programming is a process in which I use several tools. I might apply hypnotherapy, counselling or Psych-K, an approach to facilitating change at the subconscious level. I find some techniques work better than others, but I will use them all.

How did you become interested in hypnotherapy and Psych-K?

When I was on maternity leave and preparing for the birth of my third child, I began reflecting on my counselling work.

I loved building a rapport with clients and allowing them to find their own solutions to their issues. However, the process took a long time. I often worked with clients for several months, and sometimes years, before there was a breakthrough. It made me wonder if there was a more efficient protocol I could use with them, and the more I learned about the power of the subconscious mind, the more fascinated I became. I then completed my training and began utilising it with my clients. I couldn't believe how effective these methods were. Although I wished I'd known about this earlier in my career, I'm grateful for all the experience counselling gave me.

What's your most inspiring client story?

I love seeing clients develop and grow, which is always inspirational to me. However, the most inspiring story was a client whose mental health was declining, and his life had started falling apart. He was no longer able to hold onto his employment, and the financial stress took a toll on his already fractured marriage. Consequently, his wife asked for a separation, because she felt he wasn't stable enough to be around his young children.

This was a catalyst for a major breakdown and numerous suicide attempts. He became a client of mine after his fourth one. When he presented to me, he had no intention at all to get better. He was forced to see me and felt like he had nothing to live for. I knew that there was a part of him that wanted to live, and I had to find it.

Once he started feeling hopeful again about his future, his life completely turned around. He found new employment, and his wife allowed him back into the family home to work on the marriage. At the time of our last session, he'd found a new lease on life and was excited about his future.

Several years later, I was at a shopping centre, when a man called out my name. I turned around and recognised his face but couldn't recall where I knew him from. He approached me to thank me, and I was a little taken aback, because I couldn't seem to figure out who he was.

But after a few minutes it came back to me as he excitedly told me about all the great things he'd done. He'd been a cook at a restaurant when I stopped working with him, but at this point he owned one, and had a happy family life. The best part was hearing that he became a better father to his kids and mentored other fathers from his own community to reconnect with their children. After that meeting, my younger daughter, who was with me at the time, asked who that man was. I felt bad that I still couldn't remember his name, but I was thankful I remembered his story. It was a beautiful moment that always brings a smile to my face.

What is the most common problem people come to see you at Wellness & Coaching Co for?

People come to see me for a variety of reasons, however I specialise in working with clients who are going through a midlife transition. They feel like they've followed the 'rules of life' by going to school, finding employment, getting married, setting up a home and having children, yet they still feel unfulfilled. This may or may not develop into the cliché of a midlife crisis, but there is some angst that slowly creeps in.

To assist them, I created the Identity Project, which is my signature results system.

Using this model, I help clients first take inventory of who they currently think they are. From there, we slowly peel the onion skin before eventually removing all the layers.

Once the tears stop, the fun stage begins. For the first time, the client takes over the joystick of their life and reinvents who they would like to be. I often get the question, "But what about the people who already have a certain opinion of who I am?" My answer is always that it's their own problem, not my client's. It's quite liberating for them to remove some imaginary shackles that have caused so much torment in their lives.

Why is mindset so important?

Mindset is important, as it determines how you see the world and yourself. Everyone has a different perspective on things. When you allow a person to express their beliefs and values, you get an opportunity to understand if they have a fixed or growth mindset. Do they believe they can change? Do they believe they can still learn something new? If so, they're more likely to have a growth mindset. Someone who has a fixed mindset and thinks they're not capable of learning anything new because of their age, is a lot harder to convince that they are.

How can people be happier?

When I initially engage with a client, and we explore setting goals, the most common theme would have to be that they would like to be happier than they are. I can't help but crush that goal for them. I usually ask the question, "Does chocolate make you happy?" If they tell me it does, I say, "Great. I'll get you chocolate, and you will be happier. My job is done!" It's at that moment they understand how unspecific their goal really is, and constant happiness isn't really what they want to achieve.

When people say they want to be happier in life, what they're really saying is that they would like something to change. My job is to help them figure out what that is. Once they know, then there's clarity, and they remove this obscure, fleeting goal of being happier and set a specific, tangible one.

What does success mean to you?

Success to me is when you feel an overall satisfaction with your life. I generally feel fulfilled, so I consider myself successful. This is why I think success is personal. What might be considered fulfilling to one person, will not be adequate for another. Some people feel content when they can pay their bills and go on a holiday each year, while other people need constant accolades. When I start feeling discontent about an area of my life, I examine why and figure out where I need to take more responsibility. I understand that I can't have everything in perfect order, but I need to set some non-negotiable areas.

What are your non-negotiables?

My highest priorities are my mental well-being and then my family. I must ensure I'm okay before I can give my best. Therefore, spending time on self-care is essential. However, there are days when I only have a limited amount of time, so I have a quick self-care method I employ.

I start by closing my eyes and going within to connect with my heart centre. Then I do some deep breathing and reflect on my family and feel gratitude for them. Afterward, I send quick texts to let them know I'm thinking of them. It takes literally less than ten minutes. Everyone has time for this. Let it be your moment of pause.

How do you make the most of your time?

We all have the same twenty-four hours, but everyone has a different perspective on time management. I usually take the qualitative approach. For example, I can try to squeeze as much as possible into my day, or I can choose to place my energy into what brings me the most joy and peace. To be honest, you wouldn't find me using my time watching reality television. The only exception is when I know I need to do mundane things like cleaning, driving or waiting in line. I use that time to consume content. Audible and Kindle are my best friends.

There's a multi-tasking myth, that you can't do two things or more at once, due to high human error, which is true. However, you can hack the subconscious and conscious mind. For example, it's difficult to text someone and concentrate on a meeting. In this scenario, you're trying to utilise your conscious mind in both tasks. People say they can easily do this, but I doubt they're able to concentrate effectively.

If you've programmed an activity into your subconscious mind well enough, like, say, mopping, then your conscious mind is free to focus on new information.

What stops people from achieving success?

Most people will assess their lives by what they've already achieved or their current skills. This is a limiting belief, as they assume that's the benchmark and keep their goals small.

Many other factors that are influential in how people see themselves. For instance, some are afraid of success. It conjures up many what-ifs. *What if* their relationships change when they become successful? *What if* they fail afterwards?

I also find that many people are still stuck on a remark from the past uttered by a parent, teacher or boss, that hinders their potential. Every time an opportunity may present itself, the limiting belief that's imprinted in their subconscious mind will come up, and they're discouraged. Once we remove these limiting beliefs, that person no longer has anything standing on their path to success.

Why do you think so many people are overwhelmed and unhappy with their life?

People become overwhelmed and unhappy because they're holding onto a lot of expectations. Each time someone or something doesn't live up to their expectation, they see it as a personal failure.

We've been sold a lie. It's a fairy tale that doesn't exist, and too many people become disgruntled when their life doesn't turn out like that picture-perfect story they hoped for. We live in an imperfect world, and that's okay. We have imperfect families, bodies, children, careers and friends, and we must love them just the way they are, because perfection is an illusion. Once we accept that we will never have a perfect life, then all of those expectations of ourselves and others also dissipate. We stop trying to control every aspect of our lives and embrace the obstacles and people around us as they are.

Is meditation/mindfulness something everyone should practice?

Everyone should have some form of meditative practice. I really do believe we over-complicate this. I often get clients telling me they tried to mediate a few times, and they couldn't do it. If this sounds like you, then I suggest doing a body scan. Meditation is simply relaxing the mind and going within.

Close your eyes, take a few deep breaths and focus all of your attention on the top of your head. Then slowly move down to your face, neck, chest, abdomen, waist and legs, and all the way to the soles of your feet. As you focus on each part of your body, slowly allow yourself to release any tension you're holding there. I also suggest, expressing gratitude to each part for working so hard.

Your mind is the CEO of your body and being, so a meditative practise is a bit like having some time out for your mind as well. That's why it's so important. Once, you find what works for you, it becomes the best part of your day.

Why do you think people are working in a job they dislike?

People remain in a job they dislike because they fear losing the perceived safety it provides. Employment gives people structure, monetary gain, a sense of belonging and a job title. When they contemplate leaving their employment to pursue their own business or embark on a career they would love, they have to get out of their own comfort zone. This is easier said than done. There are far too many people not willing to do that and love the security of a steady income.

How can people overcome fear?

Overcoming fear is one of the hardest things to do. Fear can cripple you. One of the hardest exercises I had to do, and I urge you to try it as well, is to write down your one greatest fear. I clearly remember my own experience. My hand was wobbling so much, I couldn't even write the words. I struggled to read them out loud just in case I would somehow manifest it. Then I was told to take a good look at it and confront it.

The next exercise was even more difficult to do. I had to imagine that it came true. I had a lump in my throat and felt nauseated. I wrote down all the words I could muster and that I would have to find the strength to survive.

The last exercise was the best part. It was to rip up the piece of paper.

Although, it was a confronting exercise, I felt liberated from a fear I'd been holding onto for a very long time. I shone the light on it, and my demons went away.

What makes people medicate with drugs and other substances?

People often come to see me to help them overcome addictions. There may be many factors that contribute to their decision to self-medicate. I would say the most common, after pain-relief, would be filling a void within themselves that they're not willing to confront yet.

After some time, they realize that they have two issues to deal with: the initial problem and the addiction. Once we tackle the physical withdrawals, we work on the psychological ones, which is a lot more difficult to do.

What is the one message you would like to share with the world?

The one message I would like to share with the world is to truly be yourself. I remember when I was growing up and admiring the glossy teen magazines and comparing myself to the cover girls, I felt so inferior. How come I didn't look like that? I equated my self-worth with beauty. As I grew older, that changed to the subject of status. If I didn't have a significant title, then again, I would see myself as inferior. It wasn't until I saw the illusion dissolve that I realised self-worth came from within. It's not something that's external. This change in perception changed my life dramatically. When you truly embrace who you are, the right people will be attracted to you.

How would you like to be remembered?

I would like to be remembered as the woman who wasn't afraid to live her life on her terms. I create my own reality and I refuse to live how society, or anyone else, expects me to. I find that some people are afraid to really be themselves. They have a persona they need to maintain to satisfy their partner, family, boss, neighbours, clients and friends. I'm comfortable with who I am, and I love that. I'm not afraid to show others my imperfections. When I'm no longer on this earth, people will have known the real me, and I'm proud of that. I wish the same for everyone else as well.

 To discover more about how Sharee can help you *Elevate Your Results*, simply visit www.elevatebooks.com/results

Tracy Novosel, MD
The Results Within

Dr. Tracy Novosel is a physician, life coach, speaker and author, who's made it her mission to help people live a purposeful life full of joy and happiness.

Tracy's superpower as a physician was achieving relief for patients who'd struggled for years, because she took the time to see the entire patient, not just the disease. Throughout this process, Tracy realized she could help more people through personalized coaching. As a result, her trainings, teachings and life experiences have assisted her in guiding thousands of patients and clients to reach their goals.

Tracy's passion to help others live their best lives is powered by a vision of everyone having the tools to unlock their true potential, realize their worth and step into their greatness.

Tracy Novosel, MD

The Results Within

What is the biggest lesson you have learned?

That the answers we seek are inside ourselves. Wow! If I could have learned that lesson in my twenties, or even in my teens, I can only imagine how freeing that would have been and what an impact it would have had on my life. However, I truly believe there's a reason for everything. Now, that reason might not be clear sometimes until years later.

For me to know that purpose in my core, to truly own it, took outside help. Several factors that aided me were learning more about mindset, how our brain functions and what drives us. I had to look at my values, beliefs and the questions I was playing over and over in my head. Learning the tools, and then having a coach, were my final keys to fast-tracking those aha moments. It meant having someone guiding me to ask the right questions.

Now, if I'd never taken these coaching and self-improvement classes, would I have ever realized this? I'm doubtful. I had a good life, and for the most part thought everything was just fine. In the whole scheme of things, I was well off and had done reasonably well. I had everything I'd ever wanted: a career as a physician where I felt I was truly making a difference, two amazing kids, a loving husband and family, fabulous friends, and even vacations with friends and family. By any standard, life was good. Yet, there seemed to be something missing I couldn't quite define or place my finger on. But I knew it was there. Something more needed to be done, and it kept eluding me.

I'd been extremely shy and insecure as a child. Despite achieving goals and milestones in life, and years of education and advanced training, my shyness and insecurity simply morphed into imposter syndrome in my professional life. It's only through coaching, mentorship and countless courses that I finally discovered how to quiet my brain, drop into my heart and just listen to find the true answer.

You know how sometimes an idea just resonates with you? And you don't just know it in your mind, but in your body, your core and every fibre of your being? That's the type of answer it's taken nearly my entire life to finally achieve. It's instilled a confidence, an inner reliance, that has liberated and broken my own self-imposed chains. It's released an incredible weight I've been carrying, allowing me to use my voice. I'm now able to speak up and not care about being judged, knowing there are others out there who are just like me. If my life lessons can help one other person, then nothing has been in vain.

How would you like to be remembered?

What a fabulous question. It really gets you focused on why we're here, why we take the actions we do, how we prioritize our life and how we start our day.

For me, it's twofold. First, I want to be remembered as someone who was full of love, joy, gratitude, and giving, and was fun to be around. And second, that my friends and loved ones have fabulous, happy memories where we're laughing, playing and having adventures. It doesn't matter if we're simply talking on the phone. That call can be an adventure in and of itself. So when I think about being remembered, it's more about the feelings I impart.

When I think of my funeral, I want people laughing, enjoying stories and fun memories, not being sad. Since I first heard "I Hope You Dance", I knew this was the song that should be played and how I wished to be remembered.

I love analogies. So, memories of me should bring up feelings of a warm embrace or really being seen or heard for who you truly are, and being accepted and loved because of it. I would choose to be remembered as imparting feelings of pure joy and excitement. Or maybe like the wonder and pure bliss of experiencing snow for the first time.

What would you like your legacy to be?

Hmm. Legacy to me is a step beyond how you're remembered. It's something left behind for the next generation to pick up and continue on, not because they have to, but because they're inspired to. They can't even imagine not carrying it forward, because they see it as their destiny.

I hope I'm not going too deep too early. I lost my sister, because she decided to take her own life. I really believe with every fibre in my body, that if she'd had the tools I now do, it could have created just a one-degree shift in her thinking and changed the trajectory of her life.

That's why it's now my mission to help everyone acquire these tools. It doesn't matter if you have an amazing life. I believe it can always get better. If you're surviving, you could be living. If you're living, you could be thriving. If you're thriving, you could be creating and contributing in ways previously unimaginable. There's no limit to our minds or what we can accomplish or create.

Before, I was simply living, and I didn't even realize it. I thought life was good. Looking back, I can see I was going through the motions, letting too many conditions outside of me dictate what I did. But now I'm in control, creating a life where I'm thriving.

Life gets messy. But despite what it may bring, on a day-to-day basis, I can generally be happy in my heart and soul. I've realized giving and contributing is the key to happiness and fulfillment. We all need to contribute in some shape or form. There has to be something greater than ourselves to focus on, otherwise we start comparing and analyzing, and get stuck in that internal chatter, which generally isn't positive or healthy.

If we were all living our best versions of ourselves, just imagine how much we'd be able to conquer or overcome.

There's a book by Steven Kotler called *The Future is Closer Than You Think*, and I agree. Technology is expanding and growing so fast. During my childhood, the idea of having a computer in the palm of your hand that even children could use, seemed impossible. Owning a device where you could instantly connect with anyone in the world and have the answers to any question at your fingertips, along with free music, videos, games galore, shopping and a video camera, was considered science fiction. Now it's a reality my children can't even fathom never having. And I believe there are components of that technology that can help us with our mindset and in unleashing our best selves.

So, do I think we could eliminate suicide, and many other problems, within a couple of generations? Absolutely. That's the legacy I want to leave behind.

What is the one message you wish to share with the world?

You are enough. You are love. You are life. You have all that you need within you.

Now, I know that sounds like a lot. Probably not too long ago, I never would have believed it. I would have thought it was a bunch of made-up words and hogwash. And you know, I would have found a lot of people in my life to support that way of thinking as well. But sometimes it just takes a sympathetic or empathetic ear that won't give you the answers, but instead asks the questions that will guide you to the right answers.

What is the worst thing that has ever happened to you, and how did you overcome it?

I hesitate to answer this in a short chapter of a book. I don't want it to be too heavy. But as I stated earlier, I did lose my sister when she decided to take her own life. The emotional turmoil, grief, sadness and regret was beyond words. And on top of that, there were all the what ifs, would haves, should haves and could haves. These thoughts could turn into a slippery slope, where you're spiraling down into this deep abyss that can be difficult, if not impossible, to pull yourself out of. Despite knowing what to do, actually applying this knowledge can be a challenge. Again, I think this is where a trusted friend, or even an empathetic coach, can play a huge role. I know for me it did. In a nutshell, if I had to name what got me out of that void, it was a combination of things, but primarily it involved shifting my focus.

It changed my life. I went from focusing on my sister's death and how she was dearly missed during every holiday and in every new memory, to believing she was with me, in every moment of every day. I get beautiful reminders now all the time.

It was actually a cardinal that suddenly caused me to change my focus. The kids and I had decided to take a road trip in the summer of 2020. I was nervous. It was my first long trip across the United States and back, with just myself, two kids and a dog. I was nervous. Quite frankly, my sister, had she been alive, would have been with us. It was five a.m., and we were starting this long journey. Every doubt in the world was racing through my mind and coursing through my veins. I wasn't even sure if I should abandon our plans. The kids and I were talking about how much we missed my sister.

I'd just backed out of the driveway, focused on how she wasn't sitting next to me, and when I put the car into drive, I immediately slammed on the brakes as a red cardinal dove right in front of the windshield.

After we'd gotten over the initial startle, we just laughed as tears streamed down my face. I'd been told by many people that cardinals represent your loved ones. The kids got the irony without me even explaining to them. We all agreed that it was Suzanne, reminding us she was still with us. From that moment on, I knew my sister was with us in spirit and in love. She didn't have to physically be sitting next to me in the seat. And that's when our conversation turned from tears, fear and doubt to happiness, joy and excitement about our new adventure. We talked about the fun times we had with her, and suddenly, she really was on our road trip.

That journey across the United States was over 2,300 miles one way, and we decided to stop at every national park we could. Our days were long, and we were awake no later than five a.m. to see every sunrise and watch every sunset from the most beautiful place we could find. Through being in nature, I was able to reconnect with myself, my kids, my sister and my own self-love. I was also exercising more than I had been. Exploring national parks from dawn to dusk easily got me more than 15,000 steps daily. It was wonderful.

It was an amazing journey of self-discovery. One of reconnection to my life, my children, my sister, and, in whatever terminology you want to use, Mother Nature, the Universe or God. But to me, it was an awakening; a rebirth.

Life will never be the same without my sister, but I know she's with me. I feel her in my heart. I talk to her, probably more now than I ever did. I love her. It doesn't mean that I don't have feelings of sadness or miss her, because it's important to feel our feelings. But nowadays, I don't let them overwhelm and overtake my life. She's the reason I'm doing what I'm doing now. It's for all of us. I love you. Please know you are loved.

Have you had an aha moment that changed everything for you?

Yes. That cardinal shocked and surprised me and made me realize that what you focus on, really dictates your life.

I was concentrating on the loss of my sister, instead of realizing that she is with us. She's now my inspiration to do better, be better, achieve and create a legacy. For her, for me, for everyone.

What decisions have made a difference in your life.

I'm laughing out loud, because I've been heavily oriented in the sciences. I received my Bachelor of Science in Mechanical Engineering and then went on to medical school. I served in the navy and am science-based. My training is black and white. But I have to say, through all the education I had, I learned almost nothing about mindset, emotional well-being or personal emotional health. I had to go on my own initiative and invest in additional courses and training.

I'm a pretty intense person when it comes to education and learning. I go all-in, dedicating a great deal of time and energy. I know a lot is changing, and much of this is becoming more mainstream now. But my decision to invest in myself, in what others might consider *woo-woo*, and in a personal coach, has made all the difference in my life.

My coaches have not had all the answers. Often, they've been a sounding board, allowing me to talk it out and discover the answers on my own. Have they provided guidance? Of course, mostly in the form of more questions, which at times has infuriated me. But just like in sports, it's not the coach out there putting in the long hours of the actual lifting, running or drills over and over. They're the one seeing the bigger picture, guiding and suggesting, keeping you honest and accountable to yourself so you attain that goal.

Sometimes it's simply about asking the right question at the right time that gets you thinking about something. In a nutshell, it's about making an investment in my future wiser, saner self, so I can add even more value in this world. I truly believe that no matter how successful you are, you could benefit from having your own personal coach.

As an aside, did you know that the most highly successful people in the world, like presidents, queens, billionaires and pro athletes, have used personal coaches?

What's the best thing that's ever happened to you, and why?

Wow. It's interesting how life changes. We struggled with infertility and its heartbreaks for many years. We had multiple failures with in-vitro and a miscarriage in the second trimester. Even the actual births evolved into life-and-death situations. So, when I close my eyes, get really deep into gratitude and focus on an event I'm most grateful for, I would have to say it's the birth of my children and the fact that I'm still here with them.

Now, believe it or not, my journey this past summer needs to be included on my list.

I was on this path of grief, where it was so easy to spiral into a dark abyss. I was just kind of going through the motions of life. I wasn't crying every day. I thought I had 'recovered' and that I was living. However, I was just going through the motions. By changing my focus and getting back to nature, I've had a rebirth. There's been a reconnection to myself, my higher being, my children, my sister and my purpose in life.

What do you think is your life purpose?

You know, I'd always disliked this question. I think it's because I didn't know what to say. I was worried about being judged by others, because my answer wouldn't be good enough. But I now know my life purpose is to be the best version of myself. To love fully and deeply. To give, be grateful and contribute to making people's lives just a little bit better.

What do you believe you've been put on the planet to do?

I've been put on the planet to help others rediscover how a shift in themselves can change the trajectory of their life and destiny.

By rediscovering and living your true potential, you will reignite yourself and start living a life that was previously only in your dreams. I'm here to tell you that it can be a reality. Imagine if there was nothing you weren't capable of.

What are you passionate about?

I'm laughing, because I feel like these questions at first glance are all really the same thing, but on further evaluation, I can say there's a significant difference between them.

I'm passionate about self-discovery and passion itself.

What I'm talking about is living in a way where you're in awe of life, excited to wake up in the morning. When you look back at what you thought was a great life, you might chuckle, because it was really just okay. But by your new standards, it would seem boring, stagnant and safe, almost like you weren't learning or growing enough. Essentially, you were kind of dying inside.

I'm not saying that you're unsafe in this newer version, but there's an element, a note to life, that wasn't there before. I want everyone to have their own self-discovery, this aha moment, where they're like, "Yes! Life is amazing!"

Life is too short to suffer. It's about the here and now. One of Nelson Mandela's quotes really resonates with me. It goes, "As I walked out the door toward the gate that would lead to my freedom, I knew if I didn't leave my bitterness and hatred behind, I'd still be in prison". There's another quote that also inspires me: "The best way to predict the future is to create it". I think these words capture this turning point in my life. I'm passionate about this awakening I've had, and I want to help others rediscover it for themselves.

What do you think are people's biggest problems in life?

Tony Robbins has had a big influence on me. In one of his workshops, you figure out what your primary question is and how that influences all areas of your life. I feel people's biggest problem is usually what they've chosen as their primary question. It colors and dictates how they see the world. Studies and research have shown that generally all primary questions really boil down to two similar versions: *I'm not enough* and *If I'm not enough, I won't be loved*. I know that if you can change those primary questions, your life will be altered radically for the better. The problem is that most of us aren't even aware we have a primary life question. I know I wasn't.

What's the best way to help them with this problem?

First, it's just being aware this question exists.

Second, you need to realize that it's usually filtering how you interpret the world. We all developed these subconsciously, early in life. It's no one's fault. We've all done it.

Finally, it's about changing that question to a better one that encourages you and sets you up for a win, while also incorporating new learning tools into your life, that causes it to become a new habit.

Once you acknowledge this, it's mind-blowing how a simple technique can literally transform your life.

Whether you join a coaching program, a course, or simply do it on your own with a trusted friend, you will have an aha moment that will radically change your world. Having the tools and someone to guide you through the process, is the easiest, simplest, most straightforward way. It's so much more fun when there's someone to share it with, especially when they've been through it before. They can help show you the shortcuts. So really, life can change in an instant. It doesn't have to be complicated.

What's the biggest tip you could give them?

Start by figuring out what question you ask yourself on a daily basis, and then figure out how to transform it into one that will inspire and help you. Let me give you an example. My question was, *Am I good enough?* Although this did cause me to constantly try and ensure that I was good enough, it also set me up for trying to achieve a goal that was never attainable. There would always be another level, someone else to compare to. It assured that I would never feel good enough, and hence I would always feel that I wasn't measuring up or achieving my goal. That I wasn't at my best, as there was always more to do and achieve.

So, I felt like a failure on the inside, like an imposter, despite always being professional and high-performing. I was holding myself to an impossible goal that was constantly changing, moving to a higher rung, and would for eternity. This is similar to the goal of constantly having to be perfect. At first glance, they may seem like opposing forces, but when you boil it down, they're nearly the same.

Perfectionism is an unattainable goal. There's always something better and someone who's doing it better. You will never attain it, no matter how amazing you are, my friend. No one will. An unattainable goal is like not having a goal at all.

So, if you're walking, or like most people, running around all day, putting in your best effort, giving it your all, yet not achieving your goal, how does that make you feel? I'm guessing crappy, worthless, unworthy and unloved. The unhelpful mind chatter continues, pointing out more and more examples of how you've failed to achieve your goal. Before long, it won't matter who's in your life or if anyone loves you. The seductive voice in your head will convince you it's the truth.

Now is the time to stop that monster. To cease the unkind, mean voice in your head, before it overtakes your life, sometimes quite literally.

I don't mean to scare you. However, I do want to make my point, and that is to help you understand how critically important this question can be in your life, so you can change it. Now is the time for you to be your own hero. For you to step up and take charge of your life, your future and your destiny.

Please stop waiting for someone to rescue you. Stop waiting for Mr. or Ms. Right. They often arrive when you've rescued yourself.

So, have you identified your primary question and formed a new, more empowering one? My new question became, *How can I love, appreciate, enjoy and learn even more right now, knowing that I am guided?*

This is a start. However, you must also completely destroy the old question and replace it with the new one. If you don't, it will creep up again.

What's the biggest mistake people make in the area of self-awareness and happiness?

I think people believe that life is just this way. There are such simple, easy tools you can use right now that can really take your life to a whole new level. It can always get better. There's always a one-degree shift that can open up new and amazing possibilities.

What do you think inspires people?

Hope, goals and supporting others. I think even when you've lost hope, and there are no goals, that you can always help another human being in some way. And the minute you do, something inside of you will awaken.

Being of service is actually what inspires people, when you boil it all down. It's possible to lose hope and forget goals, but even on the brink of suicide, people have proven that they can do something for someone else. As a matter of fact, we do more for other people than we ever do for ourselves.

There's another quote, this one is by Tony Robbins, that goes, "Your nightmare is someone else's dream". For most of you reading this book, you're part of the upper ten percent in the world. There are children starving. People who don't have shelter or clean water to drink. There are places in the world where bombs and gunfire are a way of life, and children fall asleep to these sounds like you might to the tinkling of rain.

So, if you're reading this, my bet is your nightmare really is someone else's dream. Please, don't get me wrong. I'm not trying to minimize your troubles or any traumas. I know we all have problems, and there's so much wrong in the world. But there's also a lot we often take for granted. You have the ability to read this right now, or to have someone read it to you. Everything that has to be present for that simple event to occur, means there really is a lot in your life right now.

I'm getting off-track, but if you think back to the gifts you've received, did they make you happy? If so, for how long? My guess is that it was fleeting, and your real joy came from giving that perfect gift to someone who lit you up from the inside and made you feel alive.

How do you approach your coaching practice?

I have a five-step system called Reignite Your Life. In it, we systematically work together through the five major areas in your life, in order to bring it to the next level.

Step One: Why

The first step is finding your Why, which really forms the foundation of any change. Your Why is the reason your goal is important to you. It makes your heart beat faster, pulls you to it or simply makes you smile. If you don't have a Why, you're going to lose focus, and it's going to be easier to fall off-course. And once you do, it will be hard to get back. It's your Why that helps maintain your momentum, gets you to take that first scary step and then continue to take action. Your Why is probably the most important first step we take together.

Step Two: Energy

If you don't have energy or are depleting all of it because you're running around trying to do fifty-million things for your work and family, you won't be able to complete your new goals. You need to prioritize your available energy and learn how to create more for yourself by focusing on your body and mind. Of course, nutrition, exercise and sleep are all important, but the two main pillars here include your language and physiology. I can already hear you. Language? Really? Well think about it for a second. Have you ever been really excited about something, and you tell someone you thought would be equally as excited, only to have their language totally deflate your excitement? We do this to ourselves as well, unconsciously, all the time!

Step Three: Focus

We all have limiting beliefs. Clearing them is critical if you want to really change your life. Are you focused on the past, the future or the present? It's the present moment that determines how you feel about the past and what you do about the future. Learning to drop into your heart and be fully present has a way of focusing you on what really matters in life. An extra bonus is that it often seems to re-energize you!

Step Four: Appreciation

Yes, I know you're probably thinking, *I already appreciate everything*. At least for me, I didn't realize how much I took for granted. I did appreciate what I had, but I didn't focus on that appreciation. I didn't have a practice or gratitude ritual for my life and the things in it. Having a quick daily practice of focusing on what you're grateful for, helps create this love, this joyous feeling in your heart. It can generate positive energy and feelings, which can dictate how you feel and respond to different situations.

Some of my clients like to call it "achieving through appreciation", while others call it "grace through gratitude". But either way, once you really dive deeper into appreciation, it's gonna open up this whole new world of feelings and connection with yourself, your loved ones and your community. It's so simple, yet so powerful.

I hesitate to even bring this up, because talking about it on the surface makes it easy to be misunderstood or misinterpreted, but it's one of my favorite parts of what I do with my clients.

Step Five: Rediscovery

You go on a journey of discovery of yourself, your passion and inner strength. You uncover and learn the tricks and tools that will help you easily tap into your own internal answers any time you choose.

What courses have you done to enable you to get started or build your business?

I've taken a lot of courses. I started with Tony Robbins and results coaching. I did an international certification for a Happiness and Love certification with Marci Shimoff. She's the author of *Happy for No Reason* and co-author of six of the books in the *Chicken Soup for the Soul* series. Marci has also been a dear mentor. I became an internationally certified coach after taking courses with Ben Harvey, and he's now my amazing coach and mentor. They've all been instrumental in helping me, not to mention all of the countless podcasts and books. Authors such as Viktor Frankl, Brené Brown and Michael A. Singer are but a few. And of course, my dear friends and family, who've been more than generous in allowing me to bounce ideas off them.

How can someone find their life purpose?

It's actually easier than it sounds. There are tools and systems out there, but I've found taking a walk with a trusted friend and asking the right questions, helps you come away feeling a thousand pounds lighter and gets you to see the world in a new light. We have all the answers within us. It's just about taking a moment to talk about your circumstance with the right person who will help guide you. Someone who's been through it and can teach you the tools to use, so you can do it yourself at any point in time.

Another trick is learning to answer from your heart and not your head. I think Western society has taught us to be in our head almost all the time. It's too easy to tap into your logical self. When you approach any situation from the heart, it changes how you react. So, my recommendation is to grab a friend, a loved one or a trusted coach, and get to work.

 To discover more about how Tracy can help you *Elevate Your Results*, simply visit www.elevatebooks.com/results

Ben Dowsett
Rock-Solid Results

Ben Dowsett is a results coach, keynote speaker and bestselling author.

In 2001, he began his quest for learning and applying the best strategies from the most successful masterminds on creating permanent and positive change.

As a result, Ben formed a successful coaching business and created the highly regarded Universal Results System. His mission was to provide the most efficient and effective way to rapidly transform lives, thus enabling people to produce consistent, desired results, and love the process along the way.

His clients attribute their success to his innovative and inspiring coaching methodology, which allows them to transform how they see themselves and what they're capable of, while tapping into their own natural drive to change for good.

Ben Dowsett

Rock-Solid Results

What is the first step for elevating someone's results?

Somewhere out there in your future is a version of you living the life of your dreams. A life you love that's full of authentic purpose, where you feel proud of your achievements, because you've attained success in every area of your life. You make a real difference to the people and communities that are important to you and have a profound sense of achievement, fulfilment, purpose and love.

As Stephen Covey suggests, we begin with the end in mind. What is your ultimate vision for life? Do you have one? If not, why not?

What happens when you start to imagine it? What do you tell yourself? Can you hear it? There it is. Maybe it sounds like...*It's too late...I don't have the finances right now...or...I'm too busy, I should...I could...I would, but...*

I had all of these excuses whenever I gave up on personal development and my vision for my life. They were often not the best times for me.

Maybe you tried to think and grow rich, eat frogs or started with asking why. Maybe you attended a transformational weekend or practiced using the law of attraction. Or you sharpened your saw by learning the habits of highly successful people. You might have even unleashed your own power or met your destiny.

If so, and you're like me, I'm sure you're grateful for those experiences and results you created. Nevertheless, at the end of the day...in the back of your mind...you have that familiar, unsettling feeling that whispers, *I'm missing something.*

Perhaps there's some other insight or intuition you need, like an elusive sixth sense reserved for the masters or the highly successful, that could help you realise your ultimate vision.

Take a moment to notice these thoughts, but don't dwell there too long. I know you're not here for that, which is why, even though we've maybe not met, I want to say thank you, and I love you. Because I believe that on some level, you refuse to lose.

Imagine if, in the near future, you discover a *Universal Results System*. A process you love to follow, because it enables you to create rock-solid results in all areas of your life and also reminds you to enjoy the ride along the way. So, let's refuse to lose together and find out how we can *elevate your results*.

Why can't it be easier?

As you can probably tell by now, we see a lot of people who have invested in their personal development with some success, but a year or so later, they're not where they want to be and have started to believe that elevating their results, or just being successful, is difficult.

They become distracted and lose focus and commitment. This is unfortunate, as people often stay stuck, like I did, thinking they need to get to the 'next level', or give up on it altogether. I did that too at times.

So, what's going on? Well, focus and commitment are important, but there's more to the game of winning. There's a proven science at play here.

Understanding mindset: The brain.

In simplistic neurological terms, the hindbrain requires certainty above all else, for the next ten minutes or so of your life. It's thousands of years old in evolutionary terms, and its sole purpose is to ensure your survival. It's done quite a good job so far and is not going to change anytime soon!

When you try and strive for a new goal, if a specific action has a degree of uncertainty in the short term, the hindbrain will perceive it as unsafe and therefore subconsciously ensure you don't progress. It will then default you back to a point of certainty and safety, and new beliefs will kick in that perpetuate your resistance to change.

Therefore, in coaching, we first do a reset; a kind of personal re-development. This will restore your confidence in your own ability to elevate your results and set the foundation for actions aligned with who you want to become.

New neural connections are made in the brain, which are then electrochemically reinforced with a substance called myelin. Continual action or behaviour repetition eventually leads to mastery.

> "Chains are a habit too light to be felt, until they are too heavy to be broken."
> ~Warren Buffet

What does homemade Bramley apple pie have to do with it?

There are so many ways that the following distinction about breakthroughs is important for understanding how to elevate your results.

It illustrates the need for commitment and never giving up. It shows how if you focus on an intended outcome past the point of the breakthrough (or result), you increase your chance of success. It brings you back to why you desire a specific result and who you want to become, which is a core focus of transformational coaching.

This was one of the first distinctions I learned in personal development, and there are countless times when remembering it got me back on the road to results.

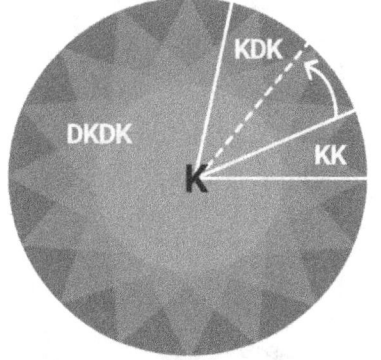

- Consider for a moment that this circle embodies all of the knowledge (K) about yourself and the world that you could possibly obtain in your lifetime.
- The KK slice represents your current knowledge, which constitutes everything you know that you know.
- The larger KDK slice represents everything you know that you don't know.

For most of our lives, we work hard to discover more about what we know we don't know (the KDK slice), so we can be, do and have more things. The dotted line represents that effort.

So, what of the rest of the pie? These are the things we don't know that we don't know (DKDK).

For example, I know I like Mum's homemade Bramley apple pie, and I know I know that. I also know that I don't know how to make it like she does. There are many other things I could list right now that I know I don't know about apple pies, but *I can't* tell you what I don't know I don't know about them.

When a real breakthrough occurs, we suddenly discover something we didn't previously know we didn't know. It's a *eureka* moment! This is exactly what I experienced when I created the Universal Results System. Suddenly, everything fell into place after years of research, and I had no idea that was going to happen.

As soon as you have this experience, it's liberating, because now you know something that often does make a profound and lasting difference in your life, or the lives of others. You can then actually do something about it. This is powerful when it comes to elevating your results.

For example, if a child is learning to ride a bike, and you want to take the side wheels off, telling them to maintain balance is not going to help. But once they have balance, they will never lose it.

To achieve a breakthrough in the skill of balancing, they must be moving and trying again and again, until they've succeeded. Without action, there can be no breakthrough. This point is a moment that changes everything in the child's life. It gives them a newfound sense of freedom and an elevation of their sense of self.

I believe the same is true for all of us. These ideas encapsulate everything you will read from this point forward, and my entire experience during the creation of Opal Life.

What about motivation?

Different things move different people. When your vision in life is clear and in alignment with your true values (yes, we have a coaching process for that), you will naturally lean towards doing what you love, and that's motivating enough.

As has been proven many times, people are more motivated by avoiding pain than the feelings they get from a win (or gain). It's also partly why, if we're not careful, we can make poor choices. For instance, going for the short-term gain that results in long-term pain, such as succumbing to your craving for chocolate, versus the short-term pain for long-term gain, like exercising. I refer to this as *mission myopia*. That one distinction alone can change a life for good.

So, here's an 'avoiding pain' perspective…

Across the world, many have suffered, and loved ones have passed. It's happened in our family, too. Times like these make us appreciate life even more and reminded me of the findings of Bronnie Ware, a palliative care nurse, in her book *Top 5 Regrets of the Dying*.

What's revealing to me is that all of the top regrets were mindset-related and had nothing to do with success. For instance, they talked about how they didn't live a life true to themselves, that they wished they hadn't worked so hard and they should have been brave enough to share their feelings. They also regretted that they didn't reach out more to their friends or allow themselves to be happier.

What type of coach are you?

The International Coaching Federation (ICF), defines coaching as *partnering with clients in a thought-provoking and creative process that inspires them to maximize their personal and professional potential.*

Transformational coaching does all of these things, but with a specific focus on the 'who' aspect. In other words, your identity and how you perceive yourself. In the Universal Results System I created, the first step relates to owning your outcome and focuses on identity. This self-actualisation process enables you to uncover who you really want to become. When that foundation is set, you will be inspired to take action. Goal-setting and elevating results then becomes so much easier. This process of self-actualisation is called 'transformational coaching'.

So how do you help your clients?

If you were my client, one of my key objectives would be for you to experience positive changes and results quickly and efficiently, so you'd soon tell me you no longer needed me. How bizarre is that? I love coaching, but when you think about it, if your personal coach does their job correctly, you're inspired and empowered from within to take the appropriate actions. You're so pleased with the outcome that you no longer feel you have a need for coaching. Now, that's what I call a win.

Traditional coaching with goal acquisition can be dull for clients, so we take a different approach that's based on solid evidence and science. The coaching process and techniques are unique and built upon thousands of hours of research and testing.

We get crystal clear on not only what you want to get out of the coaching experience, but also why, at the highest level. We do this to ensure you're naturally inspired by your own compelling vision, because it's so clear in your mind, and you know why it's important to you. When you're ready, you're ready, because you're certain that the pathway towards the result will provide you with an even more rewarding feeling than those you were getting from your previous methods. This will move you towards more empowering actions.

What is the Opal Life coaching experience?

I have dedicated my life to your success. I love working with clients on the thought-provoking process of experiencing breakthroughs. It's amazing how quickly someone can achieve and experience elevated results in their life that previously felt out of their reach. But what's really transformational is seeing who they become in the process.

The full Opal Life results coaching experience includes:

- The Transformation Space
- The Transformation Track
- The Life Force Discovery Process (right)
- The Universal Results System (below), including:
    - ✓ The OPAL Foundation Four
    - ✓ The Opal Experience
    - ✓ The Sixth Sense

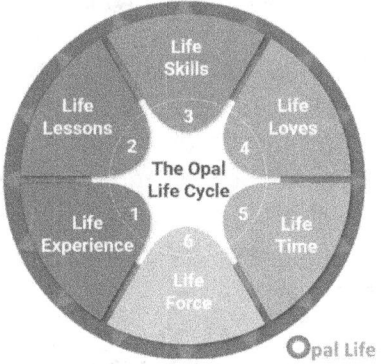

The Universal Results System

Step 1: Own your outcome

By owning your outcome, we focus on IDENTITY.

We go on the search for meaning and ask who you are and where you're heading. Why do you want these results in your life? We often find that clients are amazed when they discover hidden gems of insight and inspiration.

Step 2: Plan with purpose

By planning your purpose, we focus on STRATEGY.

We discover how to avoid the pitfalls of traditional goal-setting by using a simple, safe, fun and science-based approach to strategically rewiring your behaviours and charting your course for positive change.

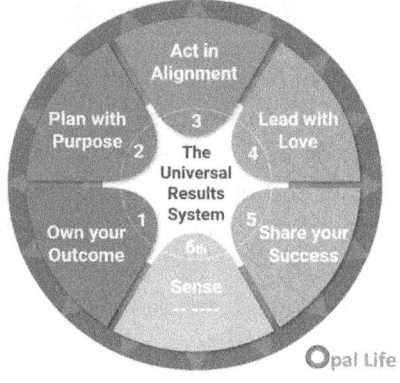

Step 3: Act in alignment

By acting in alignment, we focus on ENERGY.

With appreciation and intention, we activate your energy, so you can, and will, succeed. You realise you can apply these specific processes in any area of your life for success, and also raise your natural sense of energy and vitality as you feel more authentically aligned with your sense of purpose.

Step 4: Lead with love

By leading with love, we focus on SPECIALTY.

This is where you learn to let love lead by following your heart, in order to do even more of what you love. You take the lead in your life, because you're confident in expressing your unique qualities that make you special. You have a strong sense of purpose in life...and you love it!

Step 5: Share your success

By sharing your success, we focus on COMMUNITY.

This is probably my favourite, as it's where we celebrate your wins and the difference you make in the lives the people who are important to you. It's the positive realisation and response to your abilities, both for you and those you share them with. The people around you are inspired by your results and who you have become.

Step 6: Sixth sense

This is when you tune into your SIXTH SENSE for success, and fully love every aspect of your life in harmony.

As you progress through the Universal Results System, you will improve your sense of perception, your insight and your intuition about life.

> "There is one tool above all else that influences the quality of life: It is the capacity to take a vision of what you want and make it real."
> ~Tony Robbins

Why did you choose the name Opal Life?

After a discussion about business names, a friend sent me the following. I loved it, and the name was set in stone!

> "Opal means to foster love, passion, loyalty, faithfulness, emotional expressiveness, warmth, spontaneity and dramatic ability. Opal (is) also associated with peace and consciousness.
>
> It is regarded as a stone strongly associated with emotions, including love and passion. It is also thought to promote spontaneity, imagination, dreams and healing.

> The stone gives the wearer strength and the ability to take back control over their lives. The Opal will help you manifest your desires through positive affirmations, hard work and dedication."
> ~Source: www.jewelsforme.com

It's said that the ancient Greeks believed opals gave their owners the gift of prophecy. The opal is also the national gemstone of Australia, and therefore close to my heart.

So, what are your top tips for elevating your results?

1. **Never give up**

   This has literally saved me from self-destruction several times over the years. Constantly discovering what you don't know you don't know, continues your search for truth, knowledge and wisdom, rather than a life left to chance. If you look back, you will probably notice that it's during times of learning and growing and adding value to your life experience, that you were the happiest.

2. **Keep it simple**

   Achieving results should not be hard when you do it correctly. Look for the most efficient way. The common, simple strategies are the ones that make a difference. The time-tested practices such as meditation, appreciation, gratitude and visualisation will help if practiced daily.

   Setting an intention every day, along with a specific list-writing process, is also immensely powerful. Our clients find this one practice lifechanging.

3. **Develop your 'response-ability'**

   In 2001, I learned that "response-ability begins with the willingness to be the cause in the matter of one's life" and also that "...ultimately it is a context from which one chooses to live".
   We can't change what's happened in the past, but we can take back control whenever we consciously decide how well we respond to events that occur, therefore improving our response-ability.

4. **Let love lead (do more of what you love)**

   One of my highest values is to honour the gift of life, especially as I spent so many years trying to look externally to replace my lack of self-love. Consider how causality, the relationship between cause and effect, creates great things. Find more ways to do what you love. This will have a ripple effect of improving your life and adding value to other people's lives.

5. **Tune your perception**

   Tune your perception, the faculty for insight and inspiration, by being conscious of the meaning you add to events, feelings about your life path and level of success. It's a skill you can develop, like your sense of identity. When we take clients through the life force discovery process, we look at their 'perceived' life trajectory, and from this create a compelling, inspiring and authentic vision for their lives.

6. **Ask quality questions**

   Do your thoughts add value to your life? Do they help you? Write out a list of the most valuable questions you could ask yourself, and refer to it to guide you whenever you're overwhelmed or having a die-lemma!

7. **Use the magic power of leverage:**

Develop a winning mindset

- Experts on success consistently recommend that we persist until we win, while discovering what works.
- When you discover your own hidden values (secondary gains) through coaching, you will be able to leverage them for a powerful advantage.

Join a winning mastermind team

- Associate with those who have already achieved success.
- Share ideas, benefit from accountability and celebrate your wins.

Follow a winning method

- Fall in love with a tried-and-tested system of success that you can apply to any area of your life.
- The Universal Results System is a powerful way to get what you want. It's based on decades of my personal research and experience.

Find a winning mentor

- Seek out recommendations from others, and/or try out a free discovery session to check if you have a good rapport.
- Take advantage of free offers for seminars and coaching experiences, so you can evaluate their expertise and figure out if they will inspire you.

How has personal development helped you elevate your results in life?

1. **Authenticity**

   By the age of twenty-one, I'd been at university for a few years trying to 'find myself'.

   I'm not sure what the exact trigger was. Perhaps it was the recurring nightmare of floating above my lifeless body hanging from a noose, and then seeing a close friend walk in and find me. Or maybe it was my enduring mantra of 'the truth will set you free'. Either way, I made the decision that it was time to take action and come out to my mum and dad, so I drove the seven hours to their house.

   After a few days, I finally get the courage. I walk into the garden, where there's birds singing and the roses are in bloom. I can feel the adrenaline rush as I say, "Mum, Dad, have you got errrr...a... minute?"

   Mum takes a look at my face and senses something sinister. "What's the problem? Are you quitting university and your physics degree?"

   My nervous grin didn't help matters.

   It's at this moment, I realise how hard my news will impact them, because they don't have a clue. Then, out come those few words no one ever forgets. "Mum, Dad...I'm gay".

   All life on earth seems to slow down, like a car crash when you see broken glass drifting past you.

> "There is a crack in everything. That's how the light gets in."
> ~Leonard Cohen

Mum's worst fears come out. Things she would not want me to write about. Dad's face turns even more white, and then a distinct shade of light green. I have the thought that he's going to vomit.

After a few days, without a word, Dad hands me a letter.

I go to my room and open the envelope. Inside is a folded letter written on his company letterhead. It reads:

> *Dear Son,*
> *You may or you may not be gay, but you will produce a son to carry on the family name.*
> *Your father*

I understood where he was coming from, but it wasn't until I started a personal development program that I began to see things more fully from his perspective. I'm the last of the Dowsett line. Dad's dad was killed in a friendly fire incident off the coast of Sicily in WWII, just a few weeks before my dad was born. The letter was his way of passing on one of his highest values about his father's legacy and name.

I felt better for being honest with my parents, but I knew it was only the beginning of a long journey.

2. Unconditional love

In 2001, at the age of twenty-nine, I was gifted my first-ever personal development program. It was intense, and it transformed my life in many ways. I took a stand for love and forgiveness, for myself and others. I started connecting better with my dad, and I also found love. A year or so later, I proposed to my partner, and he said yes, though we didn't even have same-sex civil union back then.

I call my dad several times over many months to invite him to the ceremony, but he just keeps saying, "Stop asking me. We're not coming".

As the special day approaches, I ask myself, *What is the one thing I can say that will really get through and make a difference?*

And then it comes to me.

I call him and say, "Dad, I respect your decision not to come. I understand. Please know that I love you very much, and I would love for you to be there. But if the answer is still no, then promise me that for the rest of your life, you and Mum will not, for one moment, ever regret not being at the ceremony. That being said, I'm going to ask you one more time. I would love for you to come, so will you?"

He takes a moment and then replies, "No, thank you. We're not coming". I'm upset and quickly hang up.

But the next day, the phone rings, and it's him. He says, "Your mother and I have been thinking about it, and...we will come".

Mum and Dad even buy new outfits for the occasion and fly over from Spain!

So, there we are at the ceremony with eighty of my family and friends, on a beautiful day in a country garden in Oxfordshire. As I speak, I look across to Mum and Dad, and I feel a wonderful sense of joy as we're having this beautiful moment together. They smile all day long, and I realise in that moment...

I have their acceptance and unconditional love.

So, from one personal development weekend, I found love and was able to forgive my dad, thank him for all he'd done for me and love him deeply again ever since that day.

Why did you decide to dedicate your life to coaching?

After graduating from university in 1994, I spent many years trying to figure out what to do with my life. It was expensive and tiring. I worked in more than ten different professions, including a trainee firefighter, a cadet pilot, an engineer, a quality controller, a dancer, a waiter, an accountant, a migration agent, a health coordinator, a tutor in higher education and a student adviser! I also completed two postgraduate qualifications, was made redundant and have been unemployed.

I felt like a 'joatmon', or a jack of all trades, master of none. By 2015, I'd been diagnosed with severe depression several times. That's when I finally asked myself, *What is my true path and purpose in life?*

I made a decision again to re-commit to personal development, and in 2017, I invested about $12,000 that year alone on two intensive programs. It was great for about a year, and I doubled my income, but I still managed to slip into old patterns of negative behaviour. I felt crushed.

I wondered how I could still feel this bad after investing so much time and money in personal development. Why was I still so depressed?

I suddenly realised how these thoughts weren't helping me and remembered the power of quality questions from my training. So I asked myself the following:

- How can I stick to never-ending improvement in my life?
- How can I feel happier and happier every day?

As I sat there sobbing, it suddenly hit me. *I'm happiest when I'm learning about personal development, applying it and being the catalyst for transformation of myself and others. That is what I want to do with my life!*

In that moment, I dedicated my life to coaching.

For the next month, my creativity took off, and I founded my coaching business, Opal Life. I left my job at an Australian university and completed another two coaching training programs in different countries. I have now invested more in personal development than my three university qualifications combined and completed hundreds of hours of one-on-one coaching sessions with clients.

I'm fortunate to have now trained with some of the world's best, including:

- Tony Robbins
- The Robbins-Madanes Centre for Strategic Intervention in California
- The Strategic Intervention Institute
- Brendon Burchard
- Benjamin J Harvey.

I've twice completed approved coach-specific training hours with Authentic Education in Sydney, as well as their entire suite of programs at the highest level of training, and I'm a Practitioner of Excellence in Strategic Intervention Coaching.

Who has inspired you most in life?

My dear old man, Christopher Dowsett, one of the most heart-centred men I know. He's a Fellow of the Institute of Electronic Engineers (UK) and the inventor of Fastext, the four coloured buttons on your TV remote, originally created as a navigation shortcut for teletext services.

Ben Dowsett

Also, Remy Blumenfeld, who gifted me my first-ever personal development program in London in 2001. Remy is a personal performance coach at *vitality.guru* and contributor for *Forbes* Magazine. He was a prolific British film producer and format creator and was ranked nineteenth in *The Independent* on Sunday's 2006 Pink List of the most influential gay men and women in the United Kingdom.

My life definitely took a major turning point when I discovered Benjamin J Harvey and his co-founder, Cham Tang, the founders of Authentic Education. They have truly learned to master their crafts, and the programs they offer are second to none in terms of quality, professionalism and value.

Do you have any final words to share?

Thank goodness you don't need to spend decades of your life trying to 'find yourself' like I did, working in different roles or constantly trying to discover the winning formula for success.

Through coaching, it's possible to find out within an hour what you really love and your highest values. This is truly liberating.

You don't have to give up on your ultimate vision in life because of a fear or belief that holds you back. Instead, you can discover your compelling vision, develop a sense of who you want to become and own your outcomes, which will save you years of effort and resources.

You don't have to feel like you're walking east looking for a sunset. Instead, you will plan with purpose, and then act in alignment, while developing a compelling belief that the system works.

My clients learn to love the process as they achieve their desired results and begin to lead with love. The sense of momentum grows, and they share their success with those they love.

Their perception of the whole process shifts. They've had fun along the way and are surprised and delighted to see who they've become. They now know how to apply what they've learned to any area of their life.

My promise to those willing to follow the simple steps of the Universal Results system, is that it will be a transformational experience, and you will achieve rock-solid results.

  To discover more about how Ben can help you *Elevate Your Results*, simply visit www.elevatebooks.com/results

Amanda Pile
The Write Results

Amanda is a teacher, writer, journalist, and empowerment coach who loves motivating people to change the world they live in. After making the necessary changes to create her ideal life, she made it her mission to help others do the same.

Amanda believes anyone can design the life they want by visualising and writing about it, until it becomes a reality. Her passion is helping people write stories that promote their businesses and inspire their clients.

Amanda also uses writing to help her own clients become empowered by digging deep, so they can find their personal truth, follow their dreams and live a happier, more fulfilled life.

Amanda Pile

The Write Results

What have been your biggest life lessons?
- It's important to follow your heart, not the herd.
- You can live the life you want by transforming your thinking.
- You can find self-love by giving yourself credit for just being.

Always work out ways to be self-reliant. You can't expect other people to make decisions for you and look after you once you're an adult. Be open to learning new things, and seek other points of view beyond the 'acceptable' way of seeing the world. Sometimes the greatest changes happen when you're willing to take risks and open your mind to what at first seems impossible.

I've always felt the need to be true to myself. From early on, when I saw my girlfriends adoring and worshipping rock stars and actors, I found it strange and discomforting behaviour. I've never been interested in being friends with people who are just useful to me. It's always been about the quality of the person, regardless of their social standing. Having this outlook has provided me with opportunities to meet amazing people who've inspired me in my life and writing.

> "Life is a process of becoming, a combination of states we have to go through. Where people fail is that they wish to elect a state and remain in it. This is a kind of death."
> *~Anais Nin*

What does love mean to you?

Love is accepting and appreciating ourselves, others and the world around us, regardless of faults or foibles.

You may be in a position where you're thinking *I'm too fat* or *They were mean to me*. You can choose the way you think about yourself, the situation and other people. There's something to appreciate in every circumstance. You can start by telling yourself that you may hate what the person did, but figure out what lessons you learned from it.

> "You need to love and care for yourself, in order to love and care for others."

If you were speaking to your younger self, what advice would you give?

I would say, "Trust yourself to navigate your way through life by being open and willing to make decisions and try new things. Don't be afraid".

I would also tell her, "Amanda, don't hold back. Go for everything you want with an *invincible heart*".

> "The thoughts we choose to think are the tools we use to paint the canvas of our lives."
> ~Louise Hay

How would you like to be remembered?

I would like to be remembered as someone who made the world better for being here. Someone who helped people feel good about themselves, and through my guidance, became more empowered to live the life they desired.

I want to inspire and help people find their true pathway by using various writing, drama, coaching and visualisation techniques, such as the following:

- Journal writing to release past wounds and trapped emotions
- A step-by-step plan to improve their lives and achieve their goals
- Inspirational and personal story writing to leave a legacy and help promote their businesses by attracting clients to buy their products and services
- Drama, visualisation and coaching techniques to overcome limiting beliefs and self-doubt.

What is the one message you wish to share with the world?

My message is to always question and seek the truth. Resist the pressure and intimidation of others who try and force you into their way of thinking. Allow your mind to remain free to make your own decisions.

Swaying like a candle in the wind of life is stressful and damaging, both mentally and physically. Try your best to resist taking in bad news. Health practitioner Dawson Church suggests that you can boost your health and lower stress by staying away from the "foam of news" and working at developing your depth and stability of self. The Emotional Freedom Technique (EFT), also known as Tapping, is one way of calming the amygdala (the part of the brain responsible for the fight-or-light reaction), thus making it less likely you will be influenced by people attempting to make decisions for you.

Bob Proctor said that "you are what you think", so keep your thoughts positive by always being careful about what you listen to. He advises studying every day, so you're able to make good decisions. Challenge yourself daily. It may mean doing research, exercising or just getting out and trying something new.

You can't decide for others, or vice-versa. Ask yourself if this is an ownership or a relationship you are having with someone.

What is your story?

My story is really one of growing up, growing stronger and believing in myself. For years, I didn't think I could be successful in life, as I thought it was all about academic prowess and self-confidence, and I didn't have much of either. I was a genius at entering relationships with the wrong people, because I lacked the ability to be self-determined.

I kept a journal to try and work out my problems. Sometimes it was just to have a vent and a whinge, but then I started using it as a way to make plans and set goals.

By 2004, I was living in the Dandenongs with my partner. During our time together, I felt isolated, like Rapunzel in the tower, living where we were in the country. We had a dial-up phone system, and he would be on the internet in his room at the top of the house most of the time. I didn't have a mobile and had to ask him to swap it over, so I could make a phone call. Then he'd cross-examine me as to who I was calling.

He was always on a short fuse, and I kept waiting for his next explosion. I suffered sick migraines regularly from the stress. I guess it was like the frog in the pot of water being slowly boiled, and I simply put up with it. People we knew didn't realise what was happening. I was scared and ashamed. I didn't talk about it, because I figured they wouldn't understand or want to be involved.

I was working at a high school and doing a postgraduate writing course. I scribbled in my diary every day, as well as doing the course work, which kept me relatively sane! I was making plans to leave my relationship as soon as I could. At that time, I'd been granted some long service leave and planned on attending a writer's festival on Norfolk Island before returning home to write and work in the garden.

It was at this point my life completely changed. At the writer's festival, I met John, and because of my hard work, I knew immediately he was the one. When I returned home, I spent the next week preparing to move interstate to be with him. Of course, some people thought I was crazy.

My boyfriend was upset and in a vengeful frame of mind when I left and made life as difficult as possible. He tried setting my family and friends against me and visited the school where I worked to find out where I lived. He also demanded that I pay half the mortgage, while he remained in the house with his girlfriend.

Thankfully, there were no children involved. I'd been concerned about having a child with him due to his behaviour, especially if I'd had a daughter.

Because of my determination, writing and planning, as well as John's support, it worked out. In the end, all of the doubters realised I'd made the right decision and supported me!

What decisions have you made that caused your life to change?

Moving away from home at the age of twenty-one and going to drama school was a huge step for me. I was incredibly naïve. I'd never lived away from home or supported myself, and then suddenly here I was, working at night doing cleaning and waitressing.

In the first year of my drama course, I had a bicycle accident on the way home from work and badly broke my arm. That made it difficult to do all of the physically demanding classes like stunt work and circus skills.

I managed to complete the course and find work in a theatre-in-education team in north eastern Victoria, but after a year, I wanted to return to the city. I decided I would go for a teaching degree, so I could at least find more secure employment, but I discovered teaching English and Drama wasn't as fulfilling as I'd hoped it would be. However,

I'm glad I did it, as it gave me a foundation to pursue my love of writing and performance.

Of course, leaving my abusive relationship to run off with a man I'd just met, wound up being the best choice I could have made. Seventeen years later, and we're still together.

Another major decision was our big move. After living in Sydney for fourteen years, John and I bought a property in the Southern Highlands and moved there. We've never regretted the decision for a moment, as it's given us so much: our friends, a simpler, relaxed lifestyle, room for an organic garden and opportunities to be involved in community art events.

My writing and visualisation techniques were central to all of these decisions. They helped me focus my thoughts and create a clear idea of what I really wanted.

I create as rich and colourful an experience as I can by using all five senses. I need to hear it, see it, taste it, feel it and smell it. And it's essential that I keep working on and creating my story, until it becomes real for me.

Try this technique in whichever way it will affect you the most. Write it, draw it, film it or record it. Then believe it's on its way to you. The mind has an amazing way of working out how to achieve goals and make things happen.

What is your big WHY?

My big Why is love of life and the world around me. I want to learn as much as I can about people and what makes them tick, so I can help them make sense of their lives.

It's my mission to help them realise what they truly want in their own lives and work out strategies to get there by helping them find the truth in the stories they've created about themselves.

What do you believe you've been put on the planet to do?

I think I've been put on the planet to show you can follow the path less taken and still be happy. That you don't have to follow the status quo to be accepted and be a good person.

I'm here to communicate with people by speaking and writing. I listen to their stories and write them down. Everyone is unique, and so are their stories.

I've always been in awe of people's histories. What they've endured and overcome before going on to create successful lives. These stories are like a kaleidoscope. Some may seem ordinary at first, but upon closer inspection, you discover that each one is fascinating and full of colour.

I've helped people tell their stories by giving them writing prompts and asking questions that enable them to look deeply into times in their lives when something changed or moved them in a different direction. These light bulb moments, or epiphanies, focus and clarify their thoughts and enable them to have a clearer vision about where they're heading.

A recent story that touched me is Paula, who'd been a victim of domestic violence over many years and decided to leave the family home, taking her daughters with her.

They had nothing and needed assistance just to have food on the table. But with hard work and determination, they survived and thrived. Then Paula decided she wanted to do something to help others, so she started her own food rescue service, which eventually needed more staff, a larger warehouse and two delivery trucks. She's strong and amazingly focused, and has completely turned her life around. Not long ago, she remarried, and she and her husband are going to build their own home in the Southern Highlands.

What are you passionate about?

I'm passionate about making people feel important and listened to.

I'm passionate about gardening and greening the planet. It's my legacy for the next generations.

I'm passionate about aesthetics and the arts, because they enhance people's lives. This is the reason I write.

These passions are about creating more beauty and harmony, which is something the world needs. I want to leave this planet knowing I've done some good, and this is the way I believe I can do it.

What do you think people's biggest problems in life are, and what are the solutions to them?

Their limiting beliefs that trap them into thinking small and being unhappy.

They should ask questions of themselves to become more self-aware and grow into happier human beings. They need to know they're enough, and every thought they have creates their future. They can change what they don't like by changing their thinking.

A coach can help you overcome limiting beliefs by offering an individualised program while being there to support the change. A coach keeps you accountable and guides you as you take workable steps to achieve your goals.

The biggest mistake people make is thinking that other people are going to get rid of all of their problems for them, but they can only change if they do it themselves. As a coach, I ask the deep questions, so they can become more aware of their thinking, change their attitude and free themselves.

Developing more self-awareness is possible by answering writing prompts that are designed to have you look at the stories you've created about yourself. For example, you may have shame or guilt about something in your life that stops you from accomplishing a goal. By continuing to ask yourself why you have that belief, you can get to the core of what's really going on and overcome the block you've created. It's a powerful way of taking charge of your life, knowing that you can overcome the obstacles that have held you back.

Successful leaders listen to the whole story and get emotionally involved. They don't speak until the end, and even then, it's only to affirm they've heard everything you said.

People should learn to listen more and be kind to each other.

> "And the day came when the risk to remain tight in the bud was more painful than the risk it took to blossom."
> ~Anais Nin

Do you have an approach to your Writing Stories That Matter course?

Yes. I focus on using different questions and writing techniques depending on what I'm trying to accomplish with a client.

My steps for working with a client are the following:

1. **Establish what they want to achieve with their writing.**
   - Is it for self-empowerment and healing?
   - Is it for recording their personal story to inspire people or as a legacy?
   - Is it to promote their business and motivate clients to use their services and products?

2. **Discover what makes them tick.**
   I encourage them to identify their deep beliefs and concerns, such as their future hopes and goals for themselves and those they care about.

3. **Use what I've learned to guide them.**
   Based on this information, I help them create their story and achieve their goals by using writing, visualisation and my specialised coaching techniques.

Please refer to the diagram below:

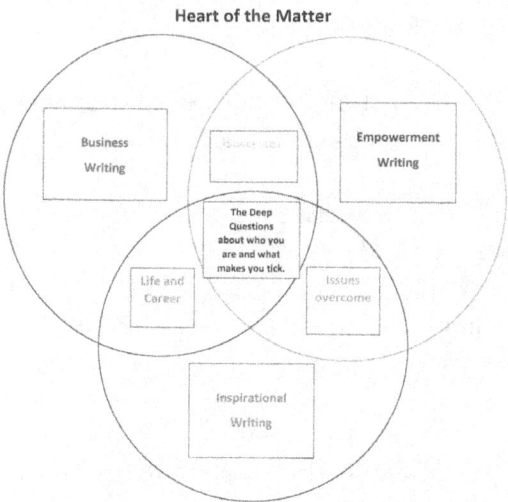

Empowerment writing is about self-discovery. It's about finding out what's holding you back and why. The questions I ask enable people to dig deep, become more self-aware and understand why they have these limiting beliefs.

Some example questions are the following:

1. Is there a part of you that feels dishonest or inauthentic?
2. Who, and what, would you be if you no longer engaged in negative self-talk?
3. What do you want that also scares you? What are the stories behind these fears?
4. What do you feel enthusiastic or passionate about today? Why is this important to you?

Writing personal stories for inspiration and business promotion can follow the Hero's Journey story technique, with the client as the hero who has to overcome obstacles, setbacks and battles to achieve success in their life and career. This method will spur prospective clients to use their services and products, and offer proof that it's possible to achieve your dreams and goals by thinking it into being. It's a technique Richard Branson uses.

People are inspired by stories about those who overcome immense odds to improve their lives and find success and happiness.

Determination and resilience win through in the things you genuinely want to achieve in your life.

What courses have you taken that enabled you to get started or build your business?

I've completed undergraduate and postgraduate courses in drama, teaching, librarianship and writing at Victorian College of the Arts,

Hawthorn Institute, RMIT, Swinburne University and Deakin University. Recently, I completed Authentic Education courses in Coaching, Difference Maker Accelerator, Success Automation, Inspire to Buy and Present Like a Pro. I'm always exploring new ideas about mindset, health and well-being and self-improvement, so I've taken online courses with Tony Robbins and Dean Graziosi, Sonia Ricotti, Bob Proctor, Peggy McColl, Ocean Robbins, Nick Ortner, Mark Matousek and Mary Morrissey.

This combination of academic and applied courses has given me a great breadth of experience and knowledge to use in my writing business.

What is the best way people can achieve a great life-work balance?

Do what's important to you. Make time for family and friends, satisfying work and financial reward, recreation, exercise, lifestyle and time for yourself. You need to make healthy choices that cover all of the important areas.

Journal writing will help you work out your priorities and specifically concentrate on how to find that balance. Sometimes it's about changing and being flexible to adjusting your life, like getting up a bit earlier to exercise, studying or working out your daily schedule. It does take some self-discipline, but it also can ultimately ease your mind, give you relief and bring you joy, due to how much your life improves.

Creating a visual diary is a fun and creative way of focussing on your goals. It's helpful for doing renovations, attempting weight loss, finding the house of your dreams or developing a new product or service. Really anything that you can imagine visually. Use a big art or project book (A3 size) and fill it with all of your ideas. These can take the form of stories, images from magazines, bits of found items like materials and samples, as well as links to online content. Keep it in your sight and constantly work on it, until it becomes a reality. Remain focussed on your goals, and take constant action towards achieving them.

There are many coaches who can guide you to find the life balance you're looking for. They're well worth the investment if it changes your life for the better.

Why is mindset important?

Mindset is what allows you to make choices for or against what you want or need. With the right mindset, you can achieve what you desire.

People often think they can't change or feel stuck in a situation and have a feeling of powerlessness. But their mindset will not change unless they want it to. They settle for the ordinary, rather than the extraordinary.

By putting what you want out there, you can stay inspired. Write it down, draw it or choose whatever medium makes sense to you or feels good, and keep heading towards your goals. Meditating, walking, singing or listening to music are great ways to elevate your mindset. Little steps and small actions every day make it accessible. Feeling gratitude for all you have achieved is also a great way of handling life's ups and downs.

Nurture yourself, communicate with people who are good for you, eat well, exercise and give yourself little treats when you're dealing with stress. Don't focus on the difficulties. Focus on your goals and successes.

> "We don't need to fix problems but fix our thinking, and then the problems fix themselves."
> ~Louise Hay

Why are goals important?

Goals are what drive you forward and improve your life. They give you strength and confidence to achieve what you want. They direct your life to plan your day. Even if you only have fifteen minutes, you can plant the seeds of what you want in your mind. On a daily basis, you can do some action that's a step towards your goal.

Believe that there are no barriers to achieving a great life. But first you need to know what it looks like. If you're trying to accomplish a goal that's particularly challenging, mentally rehearse it and visualise your best outcome in detail. This is great for interviews, talks, performances, presentations and health improvement.

What do you believe holds most people back from having the lifestyle they desire?

Not taking action towards achieving their heart's desire. Fear of change. Lack of self-belief and confidence. Many people can't visualise themselves getting what they want, but until they can 'see' it, they can't achieve it. This is where coaching is so important, as there are techniques that will help them overcome their fears. Coaches work closely with clients and use one-on-one and step-by-step processes to help you get to the finish line.

Constantly seeing it happen makes it more real. You're reprogramming your brain. It means you need to practice seeing it, thinking it and doing it, until it comes naturally to you and seems a natural step to making your dreams come true.

Reprogramming your brain happens with constant actions towards the change you want to make. Constantly rewrite the old story into a new one that serves you better. By taking a small step every day towards what you want, it adds up over time. Do one thing daily, tick it off your list and make sure you give yourself little rewards for doing it.

Having someone who holds you accountable is a great way of heading towards your goals. It could be a coach, friend or family member. Keep a pictorial journal and refer to it every day. Fill it with written and visual details of what you want to attain, and once you've achieved your goal, CELEBRATE!

> "You've been criticising yourself for years, and it hasn't worked. Try approving of yourself, and see what happens."
> ~Louise Hay

What are some of the tools or strategies you'd recommend for achieving balance?

Make a decision to allocate some time, no matter how little, to doing something good for yourself. You may decide you like getting it done early in the morning to set the tone for the day, or you might prefer doing it later at night, to bring you peace.

Using a planner, such as OneNote or Google Calendar, allows you to allocate times in your day to get everything done. For me personally, I complete the tasks I don't like as fast as I possibly can, so I have more time to engage in activities I enjoy. I make a game of how quickly I can vacuum the house, empty the dishwasher, clean the bathroom and cook the dinner. It even becomes fun!

I've used a coach to help me work on my goals. What's great is that they make you accountable for taking action. They have your back and check on your progress, which makes you more responsible and willing to move forward.

Is meditation or mindfulness something everyone should practise?

Yes, because it enables you to put things in perspective. It calms the mind, so you can simplify and focus your whirling dervish thoughts. I've found that Tapping or the Emotional Freedom Technique (EFT) is highly effective for quieting the mind.

Meditation helps slow the monkey mind and focus your thoughts. It slows your breathing and lowers stress. There are many meditations you can find online by Louise Hay, Wayne Dyer, Sonia Ricotti and Nick and Jessica Ortner, to name a few. They're specifically designed to deal with any area of your life you'd like to work on, such as stress, finance, success, depression, pain, energy levels and career.

Being grateful for what you have makes you aware of all the good things you have already and heightens happiness. Look around and see the beauty in the world, so you can feel the joy in life. A lovely practice you can do just before bed is using your journal to write down anything from the day you feel grateful for and what you're looking forward to doing the next day.

What are your favourite ways to relax and enjoy life?

I love gardening, music, walking, aqua aerobics, Pilates, dinners with friends, films, reading, drives in the countryside and art of all sorts, including painting, music, theatre, dance, and of course, writing!

How can people be happier and healthier?

Allow yourself time to do things that give you pleasure, and get involved with people and in the community. Eat well, grow organic produce, exercise and be involved in life. Do the things you enjoy. All of it affects the way you think and what you can achieve. A positive and happy frame of mind attracts success. You'll be more likely to make friends and contacts that will help you get what you want.

What is the best way for someone to transform their life?

Plan your day with the idea of achieving something. It could be small to begin with. It may be overcoming a fear, like talking to strangers. Make a decision to do that very thing, but on an easy gradient. Maybe ask someone for directions or for advice when you're in a shop. Give yourself a big mental tick when you've achieved it.

Use your time wisely, and don't linger on what you can't accomplish. Move on to the ones you can. Visualise what you want, and write it out in detail. This is how I found the person I wanted to be with and the lifestyle I desired.

Write to find clarity about what it is you want. Keep writing, honing and refining what it is, until you attain it while also taking action. If your goal is to meet someone you want to spend your life with, write down their qualities in detail, such as their personality, age, how they look and behave, what they do and their activities and interests. The more specific you can be, the better. Make sure you're also taking action to meet them by joining groups that support your passions.

> "Every thought we think is creating our future."
> ~Louise Hay

How can people find health and happiness?

Turning inwards to look for answers and make sense of the world is like switching on a light. When you write, defences and pretences drop, and you discover that you're not the story you've been telling yourself. The mind creates a fictional self, and when you understand this is not the real you, that's when you start to become more self-aware.

Mark Matousek, in his Awaken Through Writing course, says that we need to tell the truth, but we're conditioned to hide what we truly feel and think, in order to be socially acceptable. Shame can be a great cover-up for truth.

I recently attended some events around White Ribbon Day and domestic violence, and heard stories about women suffering terrible abuse and how they're often too ashamed to even confide in close friends about their plight, which meant people found out too late to prevent a tragic outcome.

Writing my truth empowered me to leave my situation before it got to that point. It can empower and heal you, too. Getting honest with yourself leads to greater psychological and emotional well-being, and creative and spiritual growth.

This sort of writing is not like putting your thoughts in a journal and reporting what you've done. It's about discovering your thoughts and feelings. You need to write mindfully and do it even when you don't feel like it, as that can be the best time to discover your truth.

Don't censor or judge what you're writing or try to be grammatically correct. No literary talent is needed. Just get it down. You're not writing to be nice but to dig deep and understand yourself. You may have resistance, but this can be good, as discomfort may mean a breakthrough.

The philosopher Martin Buber said, "Every journey has a secret destination of which the traveller is unaware".

So it is with your writing. It may lead you on to unexpected destinations, insights and outcomes. Just trust the process, and be your own guru.

When you're through, put it aside, and come back to it after a day to review what you've written. Keep an eye out for what you may have missed or what's true as compared to the story you've created in your mind.

How can people cope with stress and overwhelm?

Make sure you have enough sleep, eat well, exercise and do what you love. It gives you the fuel and energy to keep going and achieve your goals. It allows the mind to rest and find solutions to life questions. Family and friends can ground and support you. If you don't have that support, community groups can be a source of support and nurturing, and are well worth getting involved with in your areas of interest.

Many people are overwhelmed with life right now and are turning to ways of coping that don't serve them but increase the downward spiral. They're in confusion and have no clarity. Negative and limiting thoughts have taken over, and they have no goals. With assistance, they can make the mental decision to change. I use writing and coaching techniques that empower my clients to take steps towards achieving something meaningful in their lives.

How can someone be their own success story?

Do what you love, and share it with others. Be passionate, grateful and loving. Be joyful in how you communicate what you love with others, and thereby improve the world.

What stops people from being successful is that they're not doing what they genuinely want to do.

You may be in a job you don't enjoy, like I was for many years, but you can still move towards your goals. Make sure you're taking small steps all the time. Focus your mind on that goal by taking positive action. Keep a journal with your future success goals clearly defined, do your research and interact with likeminded people who can support and mentor you in your endeavours.

Success is having the life that makes you happy, which has nothing to do with how much stuff you have. Think about all of the unhappy and litigious wealthy people there are in the world!

What is the best success tip you could ever give anyone?

One of my favourite stories is the one that explains Cartesian Logic.
A man is driving in his car behind a taxi driver on a dark and rainy night. The taxi driver suddenly stops in the middle of the road to pick up a girl who's anxiously hailing him. The man in his car is centimetres from running into the taxi and is shocked and furious. The taxi driver is so pleased that he finally got a fare on a foul night. The girl is grateful and relieved that he's picked her up and got her out of the rain. There's a woman in a building looking down at the incident, shaking her head and smiling at the almost accident.

All involved are right in their way. Keeping a sense of perspective and seeing the other points of view can overcome antagonism and make you appreciate how someone else sees a situation. In this way, you'll know it's possible to feel better about something you may be upset about.

What made you become interested in story writing?

I became interested in stories and story writing as a child. I would create theatre productions and knew I'd have something to do with writing and performance right through school and university. I attended drama school and was involved in Theatre in Education, but became more interested in the writing and telling of people's stories.

I've always been curious about people and their lives. John laughs at me when I ask about our friends.
"How many kids do they have?"
"I dunno".
"You realise you're incredibly unhelpful for my nosiness".

He never knows any details about the people in our lives, and I want to find out all about them!

Amanda Pile

Everyone's story is unique and personal, which is amazing if you think about all the people in the world! You scratch beneath the surface, and you find something fascinating.

It's possible to use these stories for overcoming difficulties, inspiring people, promoting services and selling products. You can also just have them for your family to know more about you or as a legacy, so they're aware of where they come from and their rich history.

No one is ordinary. You don't need to be a famous movie star or sports hero to have an amazing story.

Stories enable people to know and understand you better. I've heard of children saying to parents or grandparents, "Ah, now I know why you did that. It makes sense!"

Stories communicate to other people and break down the barriers of misunderstanding and judgement. They can open avenues of communication and understanding that may otherwise not happen.

Anything that brings more ability for humans to empathise and understand each other is a good thing and much needed in our world.

 To discover more about how Amanda can help you *Elevate Your Results*, simply visit www.elevatebooks.com/results

Min Kan
Weight Loss Results

Min Kan is a certified mindset coach who's dedicated her life to helping women break through obstacles, take control of their lives and create profound, long-lasting transformations.

After being a community pharmacist for over ten years, Min understands that every human being has amazing healing powers that can help them achieve extraordinary goals.

Min takes her clients on a journey into the deepest discovery of who they really are, so they can align their life vision with their goals and identify what's holding them back from truly loving themselves.

Min not only leaves her clients with sky-high confidence, but also inspires them to strengthen their relationships, mindset and career path, so they can achieve success in all areas of their life.

Min Kan

Weight Loss Results

> "When you elevate your thoughts, you elevate your life."

What is the most inspiring life lesson you have learned?

When I was a child, I lived a comfortable life. I was the only grandchild surrounded by five adults, so you can imagine I was a little spoiled. It wasn't until I moved to Sydney that I started to realise who I really was and discovered how I loved achieving new goals.

I adored investing, and I believed knowledge was everything, so I went through course after course, such as property development, renovation, finance…you name it. But all I focused on was learning the skills, not why I want to learn them. Eventually, all of my courses ended up sitting on the shelf collecting dust. Do you know what the worst part was? I could always find excuses for my failures, and I kept repeating the pattern. It wasn't until I realised this one big thing, that it all turned around for me.

If you feel that you've done something similar, you need to pay attention to this part. The thing I came to appreciate through my painful experience was that until I started to align my learning goals to my highest values, everything I learned would quickly vanish.

You see, in the past, the reason I chose a course was simply because I saw other people had success with it. I didn't focus on whether this learning goal would help me fulfil my highest values.

But then I discovered this framework to effectively help me make decisions about what I wanted to learn (see figure 1).

First, I needed to identify who I really was, which had to do with my highest values, what I was striving for and what made me excited about my future vision.

The second thing I needed to figure out was whether this new learning goal aligned with my highest values, and if not, then I needed to make sure it was still important to my future vision. If the answer was yes, then it was necessary to build a bridge between the two.

There was a specific way to build this bridge, and it was about asking myself a series of quality questions that would help me construct a brand-new neural network in my brain. The bridge would give me creative ideas about ways to fulfil my highest values with this new activity, and once it was built, I could then start my learning journey.

Figure 1

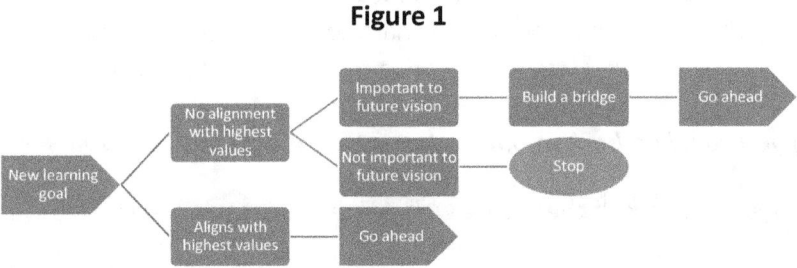

I'm going to use an example that will make the concept clearer for you. Let's say my dream is to become a weight loss coach, and I want to help people achieve a healthier lifestyle, but there's a property investment course coming up that sounds interesting. What I need to do is sit down and think about whether this course will help me fulfil my weight loss coach dream. On the surface, it doesn't seem to be aligned. But I need to look further and figure out if becoming a successful property investor is important to me, so I can be an even better coach. The answer is yes, because it will give me more financial freedom, so I'll have more time to be a coach and help people, rather than working in another job to support my income.

The next step is to find more answers to this question. This process will help ensure that my goal becomes more solid, so there will be less of a chance of dropping out in the future, since it means so much to me. The answers could look like this:

- I want to be successful in property investing, because it will help me think outside the box and not be influenced by the opinions of average people.
- This could be a valuable mindset tool I can use to encourage other people on their weight loss journey.

Through this process, I would no longer seek new courses to fill my void and instead feel inspired from within to accomplish what I was meant to do in my life. It helps me focus on my growth, not the results. But I have to remind you that it's hard to do all of this on your own. A coach will help you stay on track in a much more effective way.

If you could go back in time, what advice would you give yourself?

I would tell myself that being well-educated doesn't make you a well-rounded person.

From a very young age, I was conditioned with the idea that education was the most important thing I needed to achieve in life. If you're from an Asian family, you understand that you have to go to university, or your parents will feel shame about it. When I got into university, my family made me feel like I'd won a gold medal, so I was full of pride.

After I graduated and started looking for work, I still felt that I was the intelligent one, and I would always overpromise and under deliver.

It wasn't until one day when I went for an interview at my friend's company, that I got a wakeup call. I thought I was overqualified for this job, and I would definitely get it, but they didn't accept me. Later, my friend gave me an honest opinion. "Min, she said, "you were overly proud of yourself. We need someone to be teachable and humble, and who will actually do the work". This made me realise that I should do what it took to get the results I was striving for and change my attitude towards the work I was doing.

My mentor taught me that success = attitude + effort + skills (Figure 2).

Figure 2

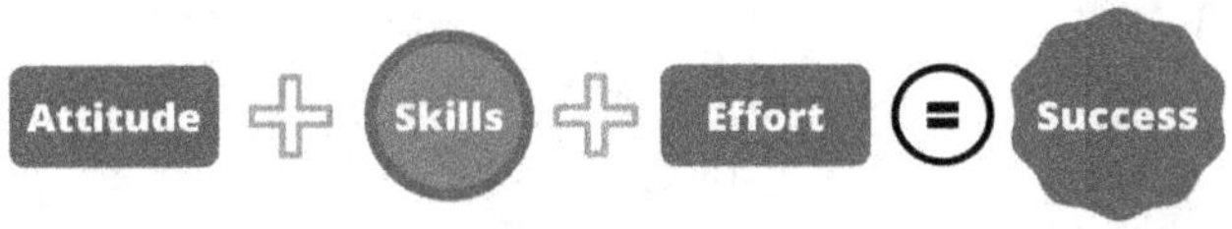

Attitude + Skills + Effort = Success

So being successful doesn't only involve the right skills. You also need to:

- Have the right attitude.
   Attitude is often not based in reality, but on how we *think* or *feel* about something. A person with a positive attitude can achieve far more than another with the same knowledge and skill base but a less-positive attitude.

- Put in the right amount of effort.
   This means that someone with average abilities but unbeatable effort, can accomplish more than a genius who exerts only minimal effort.

   Knowledge is powerful, but it means nothing if you don't take action. There's a saying that goes, "If you don't use it, you lose it". So your willingness to be better at your craft, and the effort you put into practising it, is much more important than just having a grasp of the subject.

Min Kan

How would you like to be remembered?

I would like to be remembered as an amazing mum, great wife and caring daughter, who was kind, persistent and not afraid of being herself. As someone who always smiled and brought joy and hope to a great many people.

What is the worst thing that's ever happened to you, and how did you overcome it?

There was one morning when I was busy feeding breakfast to my baby son, and my daughter was sitting right next to me having breakfast. All of a sudden, my phone rang, and it was my step mum. I hadn't talked to her in ten years, and she was using my dad's phone to call me. Instantly, I could sense something was wrong.

I still remember clearly what she said to me. "Min, I have really bad news for you. Your father passed away this morning during his sleep". My brain went blank. How could that be? I'd just been messaging him the night before.

I'd always had a dream that I would coach my father, because I believed I could help him with a lot of the struggles he had in life. But now it was too late. It was like the biggest alarm bell for me that life doesn't wait.

Although this was a tragedy, I'm really grateful for it and that I chose to look at it in a different way. This event changed the direction of my life forever. It became my strongest Why to provide value to society.

My father made me realise that nothing was more important than my physical health. It's the foundation for achieving anything you desire. He was very weak for the last few months of his life, and he didn't even know.

> "When health is absent, wisdom cannot reveal itself, strength cannot fight, wealth becomes useless, and intelligence cannot be applied."
> ~*Eleanor Roosevelt*

So I made the decision to become a coach. If I can give hope to someone, I go all in, because I don't want to miss helping another person in my life that could be like my father.

Have you had any aha moments that changed everything for you?

It used to be that whenever I wanted to achieve something in life, such as getting more clients, having better marketing strategies, or gaining more advanced video skills, my first action was to spend money. For example, I would go straight to eBay to buy some video equipment, purchase a course or program, and so on. Yes, I was an action-taker, but they were the wrong actions. Eventually, my excitement would wear off, and I'd have no energy and inspiration left to create the most important part of my business: the content.

Once I joined a ten-day video challenge to help build my confidence in front of the camera. Each day, we needed to make a short one-minute video about a certain topic. After this challenge, I had an aha moment. I realised that I was my own best healer and had everything I needed to be successful. This changed the way I think, achieve goals and plan my strategies—basically everything.

For example, if I wanted to make a regular Facebook Live video that would help improve people's quality of life, I didn't need fancy gadgets to shoot it. All I required was a smart phone and good natural lighting. What I really had to do was focus on how to find the best content to match with the needs of my audience, so they could have the most impact. This is about trial and error and practicing to make progress. My mentor always used to say, "It's not about getting it right, it's about getting it started".

Have you ever experienced something similar? When you want to improve the way you do something, do you just go searching on Google to get some guru's advice and find that you get more confused and frustrated?

My advice to you is this: if the thing you want to improve is important to you, whether it's about a relationship, creating wealth or losing weight, the best way to get results is to find a coach to help you. They will provide a systematic approach to tackling the problem, because there's no quick fix or one-size-fits-all solution. But if you choose to search on Google, that's all you'll find. It's like taking a Panadol to get rid of a headache without understanding why it's there in the first place.

What is the best thing that has ever happened to you, and why?

The best thing that happened in my life was when I gave birth to my son and daughter. It wasn't a smooth journey for both pregnancies, so I really treasured those experiences. I'm still amazed how a baby is developed from a single cell.

What I didn't expect was that these little human beings would teach me so much about life. They made me realize that everyone is born with boldness, persistence creativity and unlimited potential, but as we grow older, we limit ourselves through our life experiences and other people's limiting beliefs.

My daughter has a strong personality, so if she wants to do something, it's hard to change her mind. My mum suggests I use even stronger force to make her listen to me, or otherwise she will be "out of control".

However, my view is different. I believe every child has their own strengths, and as a parent, we need to help them to become the best person they can be. So, controlling my daughter's behaviour would only make her become someone else, and her life would be miserable. I have to admit that it's challenging to face her stubbornness, but I can see the leadership quality in her, and I'm committed to cultivating her strength, not controlling and suppressing it.

Another thing my kids have taught me is to be mindful about what's coming out of our mouths. We have a whole set of limiting beliefs and can unintentionally pass them down to our kids, just like our parents did. To stop this from happening, we must first identify them one by one, by tracing the original source and asking ourselves what situation caused us to develop this belief. Then we need to find a way to dissolve it.

As you can see, you really need to be a better person before you can guide your child to live their best life, and my kids inspire me on the deepest level.

What do you think are people's biggest problems in life?

I think the biggest problem is that too many of us allow people and circumstances to control our lives.

How do you feel if your boss criticises your work, even when you tried so hard to please them?

How do you react when a driver recklessly, and without signalling, veers into your lane? In these situations, do you get angry, unhappy or frustrated?

Let's face it, this happens to just about everybody almost every day. Could you imagine how much time we've wasted being reactive to our circumstances?

When we don't live our life with the highest priorities, we tend to let our animal instincts take control. In our brain, there's the reactive part called the amygdala that initiates the fight-or-flight response to danger. So if we allow this part of the brain to be in charge, we will seek prey and avoid predators.

According to Dr John Demartini, when you live by your highest values, you tend to have higher objectivity and more neutrality, while also being more resilient, adaptable and able to awaken your magnificence.

He suggested prioritising your life on a daily basis by taking actions that are truly meaningful, inspiring and of your highest priority, so you can achieve your greatest productivity. Then you will see that everything you experience in life is on the way, not in the way.

How can people overcome fear?

Nobody likes fear, but everyone has it. People try hard to get rid of it, but it's a feedback mechanism that tries to tell you what you're perceiving isn't real.

Fear isn't a bad thing, after all. For example, if someone has a fear of public speaking, they might think it will be so embarrassing to forget their lines or discover the audience isn't impressed with the topic and content. They probably hold the fantasy that public speaking should run smoothly, so their magnificent feedback system will instantly give this person the feeling of fear to help them have a balanced mind. The reality is that they should experience some trial and error to refine it, and practice is the only way to do it.

It's the same as weight loss. If you're trying to lose weight and have failed through multiple approaches in the past, the first reaction you might have is fear that you'll fail again. All I can say is that if you choose to remain in the same place and not give yourself permission to keep trying, you're guaranteed not to fail. But you also won't have an opportunity to achieve your best life. And guess what? Nothing stays the same. Your current situation can only deteriorate if you do nothing about it.

The problem is that we expect every strategy to work and get disappointed if it doesn't. But true wisdom comes from knowing that even if we fail, we'll still learn so much from it and do better next time. It's not about the result, it's about the journey.

Therefore, the best way to overcome fear is to use it as a guide. It's a valuable feedback tool that tells you whatever you're assuming is only one-sided and polarised, and you need to look at both the upside and downside of the event. Once you're able to neutralise your fear, you will be even-minded and become your most authentic self.

Why do you think people are working in a job they dislike?

There are many reasons that make people want to stay in a job they don't like.

1. They need a reliable income to pay off their debt. Even if they hate their job, they might feel trapped by too many obligations, like a mortgage.
2. They're attracted to the benefits, such as a high salary, a great health plan and retirement benefits.
3. They love their title. They feel privileged and have a high social status within the company, even though they dread going to work every day.
4. They don't like taking risks, and they have a lot of fear about leaving the comfort of their current routine.
5. They're worried about other people's opinions if they make the wrong move.

All of these benefits are called shadow values, which is the secondary gain people get from the current job they don't like. They might not admit it upfront, but these values govern their decision-making.

It's like when someone is trying to lose weight, but they love being rebellious. For example, they might value the benefit of eating whatever they want, so they can feel in control. Or they may get excited about the idea of going against advice regarding eating healthy and avoiding junk food.

What's happening is that they're ignoring their shadow values, so they consciously or unconsciously self-sabotage their own success. But it's just as important to fulfill shadow values as golden ones, if not more so. To be even-minded and genuinely happy, they need to embrace both, because they can never achieve true contentment by getting rid of half of them. When it comes to weight loss, I help my clients understand the importance of their shadow values and help get more of them fulfilled, so they can accomplish their ultimate goals.

One thing people don't realise is that staying in a job they dislike or remaining overweight has a huge impact on their health and quality of life. So if they don't work on the issues now, they will pay a huge price later.

To work on this problem, first of all, you need to have a deep understanding regarding your future vision, which is about what you really want in life, who you want to be, what you dream of and what you want to achieve.

Then you need ask yourself how dealing with the issues you're facing helps you move closer to your future vision.

It's important to find at least fifty reasons for this to be effective. To some people, it might be a difficult task. That's why you may need a coach to help you along the way and get you inspired. It's about opening up your mind and being creative, paying attention to both sides of the equation and facing your challenges, not running away from them.

Because the truth is that you can easily run away from your problems, but if you don't focus on finding strategies to deal with them, you will face them again and again and again.

Once you've written down the fifty reasons, your limiting beliefs will be surpassed, and you're on your way to being the master of your destiny, not a victim of your history.

How can people achieve their goals?

Figure 3

Whatever your goal is, we have a powerful process called CLEAR, a system that effectively helps you gain fantastic results in a short period of time (see Figure 3).

- **Step 1: Clarify your results**

    Before we get started, we must know the target you're aiming for, which is the kind of results you want to accomplish, such as achieving your ideal weight, improving your mental and physical health and becoming more energetic. It's a crucial step. You need to be crystal clear on the results, and they should have a high level of importance to you, because otherwise, the following steps won't be effective.

- **Step 2: Learn to discover your values**

    This step is about discovering who you really are in terms of what your life has demonstrated. So you will need to answer questions like:
    - What do you love to talk about?
    - What do you love to research?
    - What energises you the most?
    - What do you spend money on and find money for?

- **Step 3: Establish a bridge**

    Your answers to the questions in step two could be very different from each other. That's why we have a series of value-linking and value-conflict resolution processes, to help you align with what you want to achieve and love to do.

    We might need to spend a bit of time on this step to build a solid bridge between your values and your goals, as it's critical to clear the roadblocks (such as limiting beliefs) before taking further action.

    For instance, you want to lose weight, but you can't stop eating cake. Through my pharmaceutical background and research, I discovered that sugar and refined carbohydrates have a powerful effect on brain chemistry, just like drugs. They trigger the pleasure centre of the brain and release 'feel-good' chemicals such as dopamine and serotonin, thereby creating an internal 'reward' for eating them.

However, the dramatic sugar spike is followed by a dip that leaves you feeling tired, low and craving another 'fix'. That's why they're highly addictive. Once you've eaten all of this cake, your body is actually starved internally, because it needs the right kind of nutrients, so it will send hunger signals to ask for more food. Therefore, overeating is not so much a greediness problem as a body malnutrition problem. Your limiting belief may be that eating cake makes you happy, and you deserve it, while ignoring how much it throws off your body chemistry.

To tackle this limiting belief, we need to help you understand the root of the issue, and then find a connection between the feeling of eating cake and achieving your ultimate weight-loss goal. You will be inspired to think of ways to achieve a more long-term satisfaction from accomplishing your goals than the short-term high you get from eating sweets. You will also be educated about feeding your body with the right kind of food, so you will feel less hungry throughout the day.

- **Step 4: Assign action steps**

Now comes the fun part. It's time for us to sit down together to design your goal and the recipe for achieving it.

Your goal needs to be S.M.A.R.T., which means it has to be specific, measurable, attainable, relevant and time-based. For instance, you might choose a realistic ten-week goal to lose a certain amount of weight and body fat during that time.

Then we will design the action steps by reverse-engineering your ideal weight, all the way back to your current weight. Bear in mind that you're only aiming for one small, bite-sized step each time. The main purpose of this is to make sure each one can be easily achieved, so we can build momentum along the way. Some of the steps could look like this:

- Walk to your mailbox for the first three days, and then if you're able to, start walking around the block.
- Reduce carbohydrates and refined sugar intake by a quarter each week.
- Eat nutritious, protein-rich food with lots of vegetables, as well as frequent protein snacks to prevent hunger.
- Read nutrition-related books and do weekly reflections.
- Post daily in your food diary. Include your energy level, number of steps walked and any emotions you're feeling.
- Celebrate the small wins.

- **Step 5: Review the results**

This step is about checking if everything is on the right track. If not, we need go back and realign by adjusting the action steps and removing roadblocks, such as limiting beliefs. It's an ongoing and dynamic process. If the results are satisfying, it's time to develop strategies that will take you to the next level.

In conclusion, the CLEAR system works ten times better than trying to achieve your goals on your own. There's an experienced coach you can rely on who can keep you on track and accountable, and help you remove any roadblocks along the way that you may not be able to recognise within yourself.

Why is mindset important?

Mindset is a way of thinking. It's your collection of thoughts and beliefs that shape your cognitive habits. It's important, because it plays a significant role in determining your achievement and success, so if you're serious about this, you must learn to master your mindset.

There are four main reasons why mindset is important:

1. **It's essential for developing a healthy sense of self-worth**

   A strong and positive mindset affects your daily internal dialogue and reinforces your beliefs, attitudes and feelings about yourself. It becomes the safeguard of your mind and brings positivity and inspiration, rather than criticism and doubt.

2. **It forms a successful perspective**

   Mindset has a direct impact on your perspective. Your foundational beliefs, attitudes and biases naturally affect the way you process information and experience the world around you. Having a growth mindset that views problems as challenges and learning experiences, helps to form a successful perspective and achieve long-term goals.

3. **It drives motivation**

   Mindset is critical to motivation, and it has the power to improve focus and encourage your commitment to accomplishing your future vision. With the proper mindset, you will be self-motivated and thrive, which will motivate you to accomplish more.

4. **It builds mental toughness**

   Mindset plays an essential role in building resilience.
   No matter what you want to achieve, the path to your success always involves challenges. A correct mindset will help you build mental toughness, which determines whether you will

face challenges and work through hardships to succeed, or simply claim defeat.

How does visualisation help in life?

Visualisation is a powerful goal-setting tool that's used by elite athletes, the super-rich and peak performers. The most successful people, from Jim Carey to Oprah, credit some of their success to regular visualisation. There's a saying that you can never solve present problems in the present, because it's your present self that created them. This is when visualisation comes into play.

According to Bruce H. Lipton, Ph.D., a former professor of medicine at Stanford University, we have two minds: the conscious and the subconscious. The subconscious mind processes at forty-million bits of data per second, whereas the conscious mind processes at only forty bits per second. This means the subconscious mind is processing information at an astronomical rate that you're not even noticing.

To harness the power of your subconscious mind, you need to think in visual images and feelings. Let's say you want to lose weight. You're much more likely to achieve your goal if you try focusing on the mental imagery and the feelings associated with it, such as having that loving relationship or being a role model to your kids, so they can live a healthier and more fulfilling life. This is what visualisation is all about. It's a technique for creating a mental image of a future event. The daily practice of visualising your dreams as already happening can rapidly accelerate your achievement.

Research shows that visualisation works, because neurons in our brains interpret imagery as equivalent to a real-life action. This means whether it's real or imagined, your brain can't tell the difference. When you visualise an act, your brain creates a new neural pathway that primes your body to act in a way consistent with what you imagined, so it achieves a similar result without actually performing the physical activity.

There are five benefits to visualisation:

1. It activates your creative subconscious that generates inventive ideas to achieve your goal and spark inspiration.
2. It opens your mind to all possibilities. When you can visualise your goals and dreams in your mind, you can see that anything and everything is possible.
3. It optimises your performance. Many professional athletes understand the power of visualisation, as they know their performance will be better if they can rehearse it in their mind's eye first.
4. It creates clarity and intention. Sometimes you may not know what you want until you can picture it.
5. It builds your internal motivation and programs your brain to rapidly perceive and recognise the resources you will need to achieve your dreams.

How do you help your clients lose weight and maintain their results?

As I mentioned, I've dedicated my life to helping women break through obstacles, take control of their lives and create profound, long-lasting transformations. I've helped a lot of women lose weight and become healthier.

I must admit that the number one reason for obesity is appetite control. People overeat for many different reasons. It could be from stress, lack of meal planning due to a busy lifestyle or other emotional reasons. Their poor choices lead to food addictions, when the body is constantly asking for more sustenance, but they're still malnourished. This could dramatically impact people's health, mental state and relationships with their loved ones.

When clients come to my coaching program for weight loss, they've usually tried at least three other programs, and either they didn't get results, or they were successful but quickly put the weight back on once they finished the program. It's hard for them to make good choices, when the market is flooded with instant-gratification solutions, and you can buy inexpensive drugs from the pharmacy for hunger control. The problem with these programs is that they just provide a patch-up job, rather than digging deep and getting you to pay attention to the root cause of the problem, so results tend to be unsustainable.

Therefore, our approach to weight loss is holistic. When someone wants to lose weight, I first need to have a deep understanding about why it's important to them. And I won't be satisfied with only surface-level reasons, such as wanting to look good or fitting into a certain dress. I will dig for the gold and keep asking questions from different angles, until I discover the reason from the deepest level, such as wanting to live a long life, so they can spend more time with their children. If the process is done properly, the client's resource centre will be turned on, which means they will be inspired from within to seek solutions.

I will push through their subconscious and get to the root of why they overeat, and we won't move forward until I've clarified the real reasons and helped remove the roadblocks.

My next step is to identify how overeating benefits my client. You're probably shocked that I don't ask the usual question about the benefits of losing weight. What I'm looking for here are the shadow values related to their weight issues. People often want to lose weight, but the shadow values they gain from eating whatever they want could be the main reason for not achieving optimal results. Shadow values are important to my clients, but they're usually unable to openly admit them. There are seven common shadow values. They are:

- attention
- belonging
- control
- power
- rebelliousness
- superiority
- validation

My clients may love the feeling of being rebellious, taking control and being the centre of attention. Our bodies are value-feeding machines, so unless we help them realise that losing weight will allow them to achieve these feelings with a healthier and more positive approach, the body will always find ways to put the weight back on.

As you can see, losing weight is much more than just joining a program or starting a medication routine, which is why so many people have failed and lose confidence with any new approach they might take. Weight loss needs to happen not only at the physical level, but at the chemical and cellular level as well, so doing this all on your own can be challenging.

Whatever goals you want to achieve in life, I highly recommend working with a coach on a daily basis. They will help maximise your results in the shortest amount of time. As Dr Ross Walker, the author of *Cell Factor* says, "You cannot achieve anything without a coach".

 To discover more about how Min can help you *Elevate Your Results*, simply visit www.elevatebooks.com/results

Kim Townsend
Stressless Results

Kim Townsend is an internationally certified coach who helps other coaches gain their international credentials.

Kim is the Queen of Calm. Utilising her unique set of skills, she draws from a myriad of life experiences to support others in moving beyond their stress, which she believes is the major contributor to an unfulfilled life.

Using mindset strategies and creative psychotherapy techniques, she compassionately guides her clients to clear their unconscious, trapped emotions and embrace who they truly are, so they can authentically create the life they love, fully aligned with their heart's desires.

Kim is passionate about intergenerational connectedness, family, health, community, creativity, adventure and travel. Her real value is in her playful authenticity and innate wisdom.

Kim Townsend

Stressless Results

How do you view life?

They say "life is a journey" or "like a roller coaster". But I find the concept of life being a journey quite tedious, and as much as I love roller coasters, they're full of extremes, can be quite frightening to many, and once you're on it, you have no control. I find neither very inspiring as a metaphor for life.

To me, life is more playful and like a combination of a *Magical Mystery Tour* and a pinball machine.

Imagine you've just been thrown on The Beatles' *Magical Mystery Tour* bus or Harry Potter's Knight Rider bus and told, "You're going to be here for the rest of your life, so make the most of it". If you know that there's no option of getting off, what do you do?

You have a few choices. You can take a seat, be pissed off that this is not what you want, and go wherever the bus takes you, feeling miserable and angry. You can also sit in a place of victimhood and think, *Why me?*, focusing on what you're missing and resigning yourself to feeling helpless. *This is my lot in life. I just gotta put up with it.*

Or you can see this challenge as an opportunity. Starting off as a passenger with ferocious curiosity, you assess the situation and begin learning how this world works. In a state of wonder and awe, you set about discovering even more.

You question everything you see and do. What you like, what you don't like, who you interact with, how you behave and where you belong. And you enjoy the insights and growth.

As time goes by, people with their advice and opinions come and go. You become more discerning as to what and who you believe and what applies to you, all the while learning more and more about who you are and what's true for you.

You discover what brings you harmony, fulfilment and joy. What motivates and inspires you.

The clearer you get about who you are, the more you'll want to take charge of your life, accept full responsibility for yourself and design your own destiny. In time, you gradually navigate your way to being the driver of the bus and the creator of the magical life you love.

I think too many people see life as something to be endured, not an opportunity to create whatever they want. They live in a place of resignation, addicted to mediocrity and complacency, feeling not good enough and having a general sense of lack. They're resigned to a reality of 'This is as good as it gets. I have no control,' believing life is totally governed by external influences, rules and regulations.

However, when you choose to move out of that place of resignation and take full responsibility for who you are, how you show up and what you want, you can create the life you want. It may not happen overnight, but it can happen. If something lights you up and makes you feel inspired, motivated and joyful, do more of it.

This is where the pinball machine comes in. The balls are your plans. You line them up, and you launch. Some bounce around, change direction and score points, before completing their path. Others go straight 'down the guts', either directly to completion, ready for the next plan, or they're re-jigged and become more aligned with your goal.

Independence is important, but getting to the point of disconnection is dangerous. We are interdependent beings.

If you don't know how to take full responsibility for your mind, body and spirit, or how to find direction in your life, reach out for support from family and friends. You may also prefer to seek help from a school, coach or mentor.

The main point is that you follow that feeling of joy. When you dare to be vulnerable and have the courage to fully connect with who you are, what you love and follow your heart, the elevated results, joy, freedom and fulfilment will follow.

Life is what you make it. Why not make it adventurous and fun?

What is the message you want to share with the world?

In short, to elevate your results, you need to *know, accept and embrace who you are!* This is where you will find freedom and internal peace.

Whatever you do, you must remember that you're a human *being* first and a human *doing* second. What you know matters, but who you are matters more.

Gathering skills and focusing on what you can do in life is meaningless, unless you have equal or more focus on who you're being. Understanding, accepting and honouring you for who you are, is paramount.

Be aware and ask yourself, *What stories am I telling myself, that aren't true?*

Let go of who you think you're supposed to be. You're allowed to be whoever you want and to follow your dreams and desires. Find the right people to support you in following your path without judgement. Have the courage to be vulnerable, ask for support and take inspired action to do what lights you up, to create the life you love.

Life is not about thinking outside of the box. It's about realising *there is no box*. Everyone has unlimited potential to be explored and embodied.

To achieve your goal means undoing a lot of beliefs or behaviours you've been programmed to accept as your truth. Go on your mission of self-enquiry to discover what *your* beliefs and values are and which ones you've taken on automatically from someone else when you were growing up. Then shed or change those beliefs to be congruent with who you really are, and deal with everything that causes discomfort or stress.

> "When we deny our stories, they define us. When we own our story, we get to rewrite the ending."
> ~Brené Brown

What do you think is a major problem in the world?

I think the biggest problem in the world is addiction to stress, because people don't really understand it and brush it off as nothing much to worry about.

Understood and used constructively, stress has a purpose beyond survival. It's an opportunity to grow and how resilience develops.

But at its worst, stress is a silent, insidious epidemic. A slow suicide.

With stress-related illnesses accounting for eighty percent of deaths, it's beyond my comprehension why people acknowledge they experience it, but do very little or nothing about it. Instead, they choose to minimise and normalise it.

They don't know that their health problems are symptoms of stress. They work around or numb the symptoms, rather than fully understanding and learning how to reduce and prevent them.

As I did for some time, they over-medicate or self-medicate with alcohol, drugs and other addictions, or let their internal tensions build and explode out on others.

What I find most disturbing is that they model inadequate, ineffective stress management strategies to their kids, creating another generation lacking in emotional resilience skills. And worse still, everyone they come in contact with becomes a victim of their emotional or physical abuse, because they've chosen to ignore what stress is doing to their minds and bodies.

What do people need to know about stress?

People seem to think that stress is an external thing. In fact, the triggers may be external, but stress is a reaction to not having all of the appropriate information, education, communication, mindset, resilience and other skills to manage a situation calmly and effectively.

It's your body's innate reaction to fear.

The fact that we're born with only two innate fears, loud noises and falling, means that all others are learned, either through conditioning by taking on other people's fears, or through a bad experience that hasn't healed.

The 'stress response', commonly known as 'fight or flight', is the body's natural, innate reaction to fear and danger. It's an instinctive survival mechanism that releases hormones and chemicals that prepare you to run from danger, fight for your life or sometimes even freeze.

What should happen after the danger has passed is that the 'relaxation response' kicks in and returns the chemical balance and bodily functions back to normal.

The problem is that in our modern, fast-paced lives, we've transformed non-life-threatening situations into fearful or dangerous stress-inducing ones. This can mean that the stress response is almost permanently turned on.

For example, something as simple as missing a train and running late for work can trigger fear that when you arrive at your job, you will miss an important meeting or be reprimanded by your boss, etc. The imagination can take this scenario to the threat of losing your job and the ways having no income will affect your livelihood, which is definitely concerning, but not life threatening. However, because your mind doesn't know the difference between imagined and real danger, it releases the stress response just in case, to keep you safe.

This reaction also happens anytime you're pushed outside of your comfort zone, physically or emotionally.

The human body is exceptional at adaptation and gradually learns to operate with stress hormones in the system. You may not feel stressed, but those chemicals are still being released and slowly damaging your mind and body, affecting your health, relationships and results.

You have a choice to be totally consumed by your automatic reactions or learn about them and choose your empowering response.

What are the physical dangers of stress?

I learned something while studying meditation teacher training that blew my mind and helped explain why so many people have the health and life issues they do.

It actually set me off on my business path, because I could see how stress had impacted my life to the extent of total overwhelm and addiction, and I could understand how rife the problem was in our community.

To prepare your body to fight or run for its life, the main physical stress response reactions include:

- adrenalin release, increased heart rate and blood pressure
- fast and shallow breathing
- tear and saliva production and digestion stoppage
- non-functioning bodily waste elimination, where sphincters either open or slam shut
- constriction of blood vessels in many parts of the body, while others dilate to increase blood and glucose in the muscles
- dilation of pupils and hyper-vigilance
- ceasing of sexual function
- acceleration of instantaneous reflexes, such as twitching or jumping at any sound or movement.

If you experience any of these symptoms, take a moment to understand the compounding effect on the mind, body and emotions.

The body is built to cope with this in short bursts, until the danger has passed. However, for many of us, these reactions are almost permanently in our system to some degree. The long-term effects show up as these symptoms:

- Headaches, foggy brain, lack of focus and concentration
- Eye issues
- Trouble sleeping
- Continual mind chatter
- Digestion, gut and bladder issues
- Mood swings
- Low libido and erectile dysfunction

- Muscle stiffness, backache and neck pain
- ... And much more.

Over time, due to only treating the symptoms and not the problem, these symptoms can become:

- anxiety and panic disorders
- hypertension and stroke
- heart disease and attack
- ulcers and digestive disorders
- addiction, depression and suicide
- ... and much more.

Most people tend to dismiss the stress symptoms, until their health and life feel out of control. When there's not enough time, they feel disorganised, exhausted and have no calm. Damage has already started by the time people think, *I should do something about this*.

Taking pharmaceuticals to reduce the symptoms, so they can keep pushing through, just adds another stressor to the body and doesn't address the problem.

What stress management strategies do you recommend?

Manage your stress, and manage your life. Create calm and freedom in your mind, body, spirit and environment through self-awareness, self-responsibility, self-care and support.

Here are some strategies.

- **Education**

    First, do some research, and learn about the stress response. Fully understand the physical effects of it on your body. Know how stress shows up in you and how to recognise the signs as they start, so you can implement calming tools straight away. Prevent the bigger problem. Don't wait until it's so big, it's affecting how you function.

- **Relaxation tools**

These are the tools I teach people about in my counselling, coaching, workshops and retreats.

1. **Use your natural pharmacy**

    Our bodies come equipped with their own natural pharmacy. We're just not taught how to best utilise it.

    The most powerful and easily accessible tool is your breath. It can bring your feelings, hormones and energy back into harmony.

    When people are over-excited or go into a panic, they're often told to take ten deep breaths. This isn't just an old wives' tale or a throwaway line. It's the perfect technique to bring yourself back into the 'now', feeling calmer and more grounded. The focus on your breathing initiates the relaxation response, bringing the chemicals in your body back into balance.

    There are many, many techniques you can use, and it's up to you to find the ones that resonate and fit in within your lifestyle. The goal is to first manage your stress in a healthy, proactive way, and then to reduce and prevent it.

    When you feel signs of stress coming on, you should do the following:

- **Pause**
  If you can, stop what you're doing, so the stress doesn't increase. If you can't stop, go to the next step.

- **Presence**
  Take one to ten deep breaths to bring your attention and focus into the now. This brings calm. Ask yourself, *What's actually happening here?* Gather the facts of the situation and awareness of your response.

- **Pivot**
  Ask yourself, *What needs to change for me to move forward?*

Now you're able to view what's going on from a place of calm and take a new action. You can either modify the way you're looking at the situation or what you're doing. Then you can make changes that will cause you to feel more enjoyment, control, inspiration and motivation. Sometimes that means taking time out and meditating, going for a walk or dancing around the house. And some days, the not-so-great option of going to the fridge or the pantry.

If your body has been operating from a place of stress for a long time, you need to teach it a new way of behaving by retraining or rewiring your system.

2. **Meditate**

There are loads of different meditation practices to choose from. If you've tried meditation, and it hasn't worked for you, then you just haven't found the right one.

Meditation doesn't need to be practiced for hours, sitting in the lotus position at sunrise, surrounded by crystals, candles and incense, holding a mudra and chanting... although, there are definite benefits to these elements of the practice.

In its simplest form, meditation is focusing on the breath to bring the mind, body and spirit back in to the now. It's about quieting the mind, calming your energy and resting the spirit.

With the right technique, you can practice anywhere, like in the shower, while walking, riding on the train or sitting quietly in a beautiful space. Starting off with just five minutes a day can make a huge difference.

3. **Simplify your life**

    It might sound counterintuitive, but we all need to slow down to go faster. When you slow down and focus instead of being on automatic, you can get deliberate, get inspired and get going again. This includes simplifying your relationships and environmental clutter.

4. **Connect with nature**

    Science proves that feeling the earth beneath your feet, smelling the sea breeze with the wind blowing in your face, feeling the sun on your skin or washing away the tension in the sea or a river, can have deep, calming effects on your system.

    Make time for sitting and being.

5. **Engage in art, creativity and play**

    Engaging the creative centre of your brain and getting lost in creation or play, just for the sake of having fun, is as important as rest.

6. **Release tension through music, movement and dancing**

   The energy and vibration of sound and music infiltrates your body and cells. You can use it to get excited or relax. Movement and ecstatic dance are great ways to physically release stress and tension.

7. **Do activities you love**

   For instance, sports and hobbies. Activities where time disappears. This also includes adventure and travel.

Managing, reducing and preventing stress increases your ability to focus and fully engage. It builds resilience and creates the life you dream of, with clarity and passion.

Why are creativity, adventure and travel so important?

For me, they add a whole new level of experiences and opportunities to be had. They're activities where I know I'm alive, having fun, learning, experiencing, growing, collecting stories and making new connections.

I grew up surrounded by creativity. My grandfather was in the "rag trade", and my mum loved arts and crafts. I did numerous art courses including a Certificate IV in Fine Arts. I have a diploma in Holistic Integrative Creative Arts Therapies (HICAT) that I use in my healing and self-discovery practices. It's also enhanced my skills delivering workshops based on the teachings of Dr Brené Brown. I feel privileged to be one of few coaches to be a trained facilitator of her Daring Way and Rising Strong programs.

I so often hear people say, "Oh, I'm not creative!" That's a total lie they tell themselves. They just don't understand the scope of what creativity is. We all need it to problem-solve, so you engage in it every day!

Here are some definitions that are helpful for igniting your creative spark.

- **Creativity** is the act of turning new and imaginative ideas into reality.
- **Play** is purposeless, all-consuming and fun. Play and laughter are scientifically proven to have massive health benefits.
- **Adventure** is defined as "an unusual and exciting, daring or risky experience".
- **Travel,** to me, is the combination of all of these in action.

Think about how kids discover their world through creativity and play, combined with an instinctual curiosity. They're all core elements of learning and growth.

At some time in life, you're told to "grow up", which seems to take away your playfulness for the sake of being more 'adult'. However, creativity and play are intrinsic elements of a fulfilling life and managing and reducing stress.

> "We don't stop playing because we grow old.
> We grow old because we stop playing."
> ~George Bernard Shaw

Why not combine them with adventure and travel to create the ultimate in experience and wonder?

My travels to The Congo to climb with the mountain gorillas, and to Kenya and India, where I participated in art projects in orphanages, are some of the highlights of my life.

On my adventure retreats, I combine all of these. Travelling isn't about ticking the tourist attraction boxes. It's about new experiences. I find an 'insider' and go deep into local life and culture. And when I can, I also contribute to the community.

The world is an amazing place. And so are the people in it!

> "When play is denied over the long term, our mood darkens. We lose our sense of optimism, and we become hedonic or incapable of feeling sustained pleasure."
> ~Stuart M. Brown Jr.

How can someone simplify their life?

It's a common practice in problem-solving, or when creating a big project, that you break everything down into bite-sized chunks. This makes everything easier. So, what if you were to treat your life as a project that requires management? How would you break it down into smaller chunks?

I like to simplify things, and where possible, work with the rule of three.

I think that life fits into three main categories, which all have sub-categories that can also be broken down into smaller and smaller sections of threes.

The three main categories are as follows:
1. **Health**: mind, body and spirit
2. **Relationships**: with self, others and the environment
3. **Finances**: incoming, outgoing and growth

This strategy is handy for managing your life or planning a big event, project or holiday. Start off with the three key points, and dissect them by getting more and more detailed. Begin your action-taking with the smaller tasks, before building up to achieve the larger goal.

It's also about prioritising and managing your time and space. De-clutter your physical environment, your time schedule, and most importantly, your emotional baggage.

Do you have a system that reignites your life and elevates your results?

What I've found is that you can't successfully get results in any area of life if you're stressed and in overwhelm. Before you tackle your goals for the future, you need to have your present grounded and under control.

With any goal or problem, I use and teach the following steps. It works for stress and for whatever else you want to achieve in life.

Once you understand the system, sometimes you can fly through it to find your solution. Other times, the problem may be more complex and will require your undivided focus and attention to discover all that's to be seen.

What you focus on expands. This means if you focus on the problem, it gets bigger, so focus on a solution.

You can use this system for a specific problem or your life in general. I call it The Freedom System.

The Freedom System

All steps are interrelated and interdependent.

When you begin change work, Self-awareness is the first step, followed by Self-responsibility, to then build your foundation of Self-care and Support.

Once you embody the process and have a stable foundation of Self-care and Support, when challenges arise, you can jump in at any step.

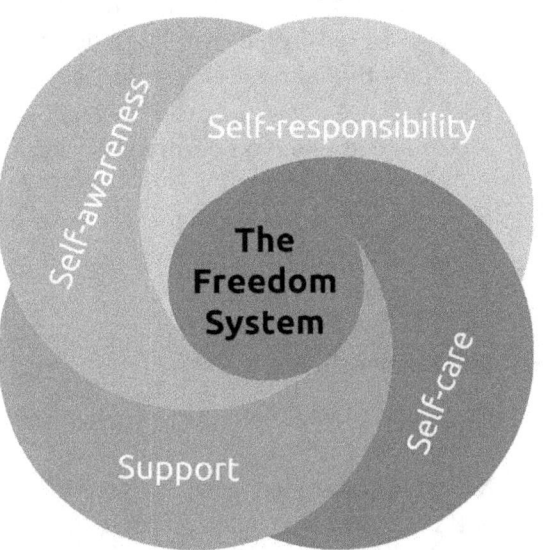

The goal is to permanently practice all steps.

Self-care with support is your foundation. Then when life isn't going as well as you may like, you increase your focus on self-awareness and self-responsibility to get back on track.

- **Self-Awareness**

    Like any project or problem, you need to know your starting point. What exactly are the facts of the situation?

    ▸ This is like a self-audit to get a diagnosis. Know what makes you tick and what will support you to elevate your results. It's an ongoing, lifelong process, because as you grow, your needs, desires and values change.

- ▸ People often wonder what makes others tick. How often have you looked inside to fully understand what makes you tick? Doing this without judgement is the key.
- ▸ Start researching yourself today! Buy a journal of some kind, and note what you observe to discover who you really are and how you operate.
- ▸ Understand the mechanics of your body and how you think, feel and act. How you make decisions. How you communicate. Unpack everything.

- **Self-Responsibility**

If you don't look after yourself, who will?

Now that you understand how your mind, body and spirit behave, you can start managing yourself, so you can make choices and change what you do and where your life goes.

- ▸ Look at all of the information you've gathered.
- ▸ What do you dislike and want to change?
- ▸ What do you want to create or further develop?
- ▸ Do you need to learn more about health, well-being, mindset, communication or something else? Do you need further education to attain new practical skills?
- ▸ Take action on your new decisions.

- **Self-Care**

This is like being an effective general manager of your own life, always looking out for what's best for you. Self-care is about examining all of the aspects of your being and your life, and how they're interplaying.

- ▸ Are they a finely tuned machine, working efficiently and effortlessly?
- ▸ Are you caring for your physical and emotional being, mind, body and spirit? Are you keeping your "vehicle of life" in peak condition?

- Are you making decisions and taking action from a growth mindset? Such as turning challenges into opportunities?
- Are you listening to your 'body barometer'? When there's discomfort, your body is saying, "Pay attention here. Learn and grow".
- Learn to recognise and trust your intuition.
- Know when to reach out for support.

- **Support**

    We're interdependent beings, wired for connection, and we need the support of others.

    - Asking for assistance is not a weakness. It's a necessity. You can't get through life without the support of others and the community. Learn to ask for what you need and want.
    - If the action-taking isn't happening, reach out for help.
    - Depending on the problem or goal, your support could be family, your partner, a friend, work colleague or a professional. Find the appropriate, empowering people to move you through the troughs and towards your goal.

What else is important about BEING?

Self-empowerment, progress and success are found through authentic communication, meaningful connection and supportive collaboration. What I call *Connectication*. These three elements are what keep communities going, and it's the community that supports us as individuals.

- **Communication**

    - Authentic, clear, open, honest and supportive communication with yourself, others and the world you live in, is essential.
    - We're often our own worst bullies. We're self-critical and hard on ourselves. Self-compassion is absolutely necessary. Learn

- to accept yourself for who you are, and love your unique, perfect imperfect self. Accept others for who they are, as well.
  - Practice "ordinary courage", which means having the courage to be vulnerable and speak from your heart without judgement, despite any fear. Neutralise or let go of shame, guilt and the "not good enoughs". It's one of the most challenging and rewarding behaviours to learn and embody.

- **Connection**
  - Communication is your tool for connection. The braver you can be with communicating your feelings with selected supportive individuals or groups, the deeper the connections that are developed.
  - As humans, we're hardwired for connection to ourselves, with others and to the world we live in. Discovering, creating and nurturing these connections is what keeps us alive and assists our growth. The shared experiences, the belonging, the support and the love, are what we all seek.

- **Collaboration**
  - We're communal beings who require the support of each other and the community in order to thrive. Collaborating with others towards a goal or for reinforcement is a necessity. As they say, "Teamwork makes the dream work".
  - Instead of looking for competition where there's a winner and a loser, look for collaboration where everyone can win.

- **Community**
  - Community consists of the young, the old, women and men, and everyone in between. We all have different needs, strengths and weaknesses, beliefs and values. Learn how to accept, nurture and embrace them.

▸ Community is what holds us all together and is the outcome of communication, connection and collaboration. Support your community, and it will support you.

What is your WHY?

Looking back at my life, I see that there was a big gap in my education. The focus was on *doing* and didn't include *being*. What I mean is that my skills and abilities grew, but my emotions and feelings were dismissed and neglected.

I had perfected looking confident and being capable of doing things to feel accepted and belong. However, on the inside I often had a knot in my belly and a rock in my throat, and I was petrified of speaking up. When it came to expressing myself, I was often the quiet one on the sidelines, going with the flow and not really standing for anything.

This was a reflection of my being. Learning to accept, understand and deal with emotions and feelings, was not on the education agenda. So consequently, I didn't learn the language of how to communicate feelings and emotions or work with them. Instead, I was taught how to suppress them. How to not get too excited or upset, but to suck it up and soldier on. Not having the tools to speak up and ask for what I wanted, I felt unheard, not good enough and like I didn't matter. This led to feeling shut down, disconnected and unloved. My self-worth was non-existent.

My disconnection to self and lack of a purpose in life, took me down a path of drug addiction. While going through a long-term residential drug rehab program with my five-month-old daughter to care for, I learned that I kept myself safe and blocked my feelings by keeping busy *doing*.

Kim Townsend

In my attempts to find fulfilment in a career path, I scrolled through failed businesses and more than fifty jobs, from nursing to fruit picking; retail to hospitality; drug and alcohol prevention in youth hostels and crisis centres to sales repping selling hardware. I was also a teacher's aide in public schools and a caterer for film crews on TV commercials. I was not afraid of change. This was what I now proudly call my 'lifestyle and next shiny object' career path.

When I discovered the personal development industry, my life finally made sense. I understood why at forty-five years old, with a truckload of work and life skills, I felt overwhelmed, lost and without direction.

I realised that my low sense of self-worth, fulfilment and belonging came from my inadequate emotional intelligence and emotional resilience skills, an absence of courage to accept myself for who I was and a lack of trust in myself. My non-acceptance of being me.

I discovered the key to fun, freedom and fulfilment was having the courage to venture into a place of vulnerability, remove my safety masks and be unapologetically me, accepting myself for who I was; my perfectly imperfect self. This was where real growth began and continues to grow. A *game*, not a *work* in progress.

So, that's why my mission is teaching others to accept and embrace who they are through healing the traumas that are causing stress and to 'find themselves' sooner, rather than later.

The more people who can unapologetically be themselves, communicate from their heart, connect on a meaningful level and collaboratively support each other, the better the world will be. In the end, having a planet with more contented, fulfilled people living a wholehearted life they love, working in harmony, will positively affect organisational change.

I want to do my best to ensure no child grows up feeling dismissed and unloved, because their parents were too busy and stressed, constantly *doing*, or didn't have the skills to *be* or teach *being*. I also want to support adults and elevate their life and results by learning how to just be.

> "Let go of who you think you should be,
> and embrace who you are!"
> ~Dr Brené Brown

How would you like to be remembered?

As a courageous woman of integrity and heart, who cared and lived life to the fullest. As a compassionate, inspired daughter, a grounded, calm, supportive mum and a wise, fun, playful nanna. A maverick who loved creativity, adventure and travel, and a community member who made a difference.

> "Life is a dance between vulnerability and courage.
> Dare to dance."
> ~Kim Townsend

 To discover more about how Kim can help you *Elevate Your Results*, simply visit www.elevatebooks.com/results

Dave Parry
Fast-Track your Finances

Dave Parry is an accomplished finance consultant, passionate educator and wealth coach, inspiring and enabling everyday Australians to achieve their own sense of financial freedom.

With his two systems, The Cash Flow Conundrum and The Five Pillars to Wealth, Dave makes finance fun and memorable. His content is based on hundreds of consultations, as well as his own extraordinary personal journey, all of which has helped him develop simple, safe strategies regarding finance, debt reduction, tax awareness, property investing and the psychology of money.

Dave's mission is assisting hard-working Australians to become debt-free, so they can live a life of freedom and have incredible peace of mind that they're growing a sound future for themselves, as well as their loved ones.

Dave Parry

Fast-Track your Finances

The Cash Flow Conundrum™ and the Five Pillars to Wealth™

When you were growing up, what were your thoughts surrounding money?

Growing up in an unknown, undeveloped suburb in the middle of nowhere in the 1970s, I probably never really thought much about money. And yet when I look back, I realise that the concept of money was often confusing.

Like most kids, my sister and I got a small bit of pocket change once a week that would quickly be spent on lollies at the local store on a Friday. This is back when ten cents would get you a mixed bag of lollies, and cobbers were two for one cent! My dad had just built a two-storey home 'on the cheap' in the middle of nowhere, in an unknown coastal suburb that my Grandpa Cliffy had given him. Cliffy had apparently bought a bunch of blocks for cash on a whim from a mate in his bowling club. He sold most of them, made some money and gave one to Dad. This means we lived in a brand-new two-storey home, but it took years to finish off to a comfortable level, so it never really felt brand new.

I remember having scattered green carpet tiles covering most of the floor, but there were patches of cold concrete in the kitchen and living room. The yard was huge, but for years it was mostly dirt and weeds, with a homemade 'jungle gym' and wooden planks to play on. It was great, but to me it never felt like anything fancy.

How did your parents influence your views on money?

Mum was a teacher and a '10 Pound Pom'. At the age of twelve, she and her family came by boat to Perth from a post-war-torn England. Mum was impacted deeply by the war in England. She was shipped out to a cousin's farm to avoid the bombing and experienced food rationing firsthand. She used to tell us stories of sharing one egg for supper with her cousin Tom, while her mum (my nana) went without.

This war-ration mindset stayed with her and my nana in many ways. It appeared in our weekly low-budget meals so much, that my sister and I would tease her mercilessly. We'd say, "You know, Mum, the war is over". And yet these days, I have to say that I learned some great lessons about frugality and saving from Mum and Nana. But at the time, it was confusing having a big house and yet being served budget meals every night.

In the early days, Mum made a lot of toys for us. "There's no need for a frisbee", she'd say, when an ice-cream container lid would do. Or "You don't need a Batman action figure", when a mask drawn using a black pen that was placed on a wooden peg with a glued-on cape was "close enough".

And yet, amid all of this frugal living, I kept thinking, *Dad is a doctor... and aren't doctors supposed to be rich?*

How did those mixed messages about money affect your view of wealth?

According to some of my mates, we were 'rich', simply because Dad was a doctor, and we lived in a two-storey house. But then why did my mates' houses have carpet on the floor and their yards have grass? Most of them got new toys for birthdays. Not ice-cream-lid frisbees and wooden pegs dressed as Batman!

What my mates didn't know, and I didn't appreciate at the time, was that Dad worked for the health department on a good salary, but nowhere near what most doctors earned. Dad chose to serve, forgoing a bigger salary for greater satisfaction, and years later was awarded the Order of Australia for his service to the paediatric community. This noble concept of serving became deeply embedded in me and has forged many parts of my journey and work.

Almost everything was done cheaply, from Mum and Dad's homemade bed they kept for over twenty years, to budget holidays in caravans and bulk-buying food with our local church co-op. We also had basic Toyota Corollas and only one television. But we went to Europe three times, and all I wanted to ask was, "Hey, do we have money, or don't we?"

Was there a major event or two that shaped your life?

Yes, there were a few, and my story begins in high school. I did pretty well, was a bit of an all-rounder and presumed that studying medicine or physio would be a sound option for me. I studied hard and played hard, but something went wrong. I did get the year 12 drama prize, but I not only missed out on medicine by a mile, I didn't get into physio either. Somewhat disillusioned, I resigned myself to a year of Science-Phys Ed at UWA, that was known to be a second-chance, back-door entrance to physio, or maybe medicine.

But in my third week at uni, I had a bad bike accident. I can remember making a split-second decision whether to skid and hit side-on with my shoulder, or keep going, put my *ju-jitsu* skills to practice and try to jump stuntman-style over the car. But as I had no helmet on, I deliberately slid and skidded, hoping for the best, and then...*smash!*

I hit sideways, taking the brunt of the collision with my right shoulder literally exploding the front passenger door. I was thrown off my bike and over the hood of the car, before waking up under a car bumper bar, covered in glass and blood, with worried passers-by telling me to lie still until the ambulance arrived.

I'd been lucky...very lucky.

As a result of the injuries and recovery, science phys-ed lost some of its appeal. I was forced to pass my tennis practical exam left-handed and struggled on through the rest of the year somewhat aimlessly, so I pulled out of uni at the end of that year.

Could you go into more detail about your wealth and property journey?

Soon after my accident, a friend mentioned I could probably get some compensation money though the mandatory third-party insurance I didn't even know I'd been paying for with my driver's licence. A young lawyer at my church gave me some help, and about a year later, I had a small fortune of $7,000, which is the equivalent of about a third of a year's wages at that time.

Now, what do most eighteen-year-old blokes want to do with their money? Buy cars! But even though seven thousand dollars was a fair bit, it wasn't enough for a brand-new red Mitsubishi Cordia Turbo, which was one of the hottest cars at the time.

By this stage, the coastal suburb we lived in was no longer surrounded by bush, and it certainly wasn't in the middle of nowhere anymore. It had become quite a sought-after place to live, being close to two of Perth's best beaches, a golf course and prestigious private schools.

For some reason, the story of Grandpa Cliffy buying land in the middle of nowhere suddenly appealed to me. So that's what I did. I used the money to buy my first block of land, which was located on the coast north of Perth, in another new-ish, relatively undeveloped suburb.

Over the next few years, I worked as a cleaner, landscape gardener, abseil instructor, roustabout and sheep pen boy. I also worked on the wheat bins up north WA, directed a performing arts company and eventually went back to uni, where I did a year of drama teaching and finally ended up with a degree from WAAPA. I was fortunate enough to be a part of the elite musical theatre program at the same time the now legendary Hugh Jackman was there.

I didn't have to wait too long before that $7,000 block of land turned into $25,000, and without realising it, I'd started experiencing firsthand the concepts of leverage, using other people's money, depreciation and the beginnings of wealth creation. And I was kinda hooked.

I went on to work in the government school system as a counsellor and youth chaplain for little to no money and continued to do a whole lot of stuff with property that included buying, selling, sub-dividing, borrowing massive amounts and learning incredible lessons.

When I met Jasmine, my gorgeous wife of over twenty years, we kept paying down our debts and investing more. We built our own two-storey home, and at thirty-eight years old, with three young kids, I found myself debt free.

How did becoming debt-free at such a young age, change your life?

It gave us both freedom and choice. I quit chaplaincy and focused fulltime on my growing finance business. Jasmine was able to concentrate on being the best mum and volunteered her time as a sought-after developmental psychologist, working with the most troubled kids at our local primary school. She's amazing.

It also allowed our family to enjoy incredible holidays. While the kids were young, we made sure to visit various parts of Southeast Asia, often twice a year. I was also able to go on amazing surfing trips with my mates to Indonesia and make regular journeys down south to the Margaret River region. We've been truly fortunate and blessed.

What motivated you to become a wealth coach?

First. there's Grandpa Cliffy.

Back when I graduated from WAAPA, he died, and I was honoured to be asked by my beloved gran to run the funeral, a tough but special task. Cliffy was known to always have money. He kept a mysterious black box under his bed that we figured was his personal bank. But when it was opened, we discovered there was barely enough to cover the funeral expenses. The will was read, and I found out I inherited a few small shares, which I still have today. My gran was basically left with nothing but the house and no money or income.

I was dumfounded. Cliffy had been wealthy. Where did it go? What went wrong?

I would never find out until much later.

Second, is my chaplaincy experience.

After thirteen years of working as a chaplain, I found I was having more and more conversations with staff and parents about money and financial stress, and they were fascinated with what I'd been able to do with property on a low salary. They wanted to know how I did it. So, I went back to school, got a cert 4 and diploma in financial services and started my own company, where I worked initially as a mortgage broker and then more as a finance consultant.

Third, was my need to help people.

In many ways, I'm still a counsellor/coach, but now my conversations are focused on money, mindset and finances. Over the years, I've found that mindset is one important part of the conversation, but not the major piece of the puzzle.

Imagining a better future, picturing yourself wealthy and feeling good, is brilliant, but only goes so far. If your bank account is constantly empty, it's hard to get motivated. *Action* is the all-empowering second part of the equation, because actions elevate your results.

Seeing your bank account grow is real and tangible. Watching your debts disappear is empowering, and your mindset naturally changes. Good results bring empowering feelings, which in turn bring empowering thoughts and more empowering action, which brings better results, and the cycle continues towards better and better successes.

What does it mean to be wealthy?

My definition? A wealthy life means living abundantly and fulfilled with a sense of purpose, choice and freedom.

Wealth gives you choice. More choice gives you more freedom to decide what you do, with whom, when and for how long. But you can only get that choice and freedom when you're financially secure. You need to have more money at the end of the month, rather than more month at the end of your money! And ultimately, you need to get to the stage where your money is working for you, rather than you working for it.

But there's more to the equation than that. It's not just about the money. It's about being fulfilled and finding contentment. Over my lifetime, I've met people with a lot of money who are generous, content, driven to make change in the world and live a life of fulfilment and contribution. But I've also encountered those who are just plain miserable. I've talked to people with little to no money who are angry, resentful and not in a good place, while others in the same situation are among the most contented and generous people you could ever meet.

So let me share with you my secret thought. There are usually only two ways to be wealthy.

1. Having everything you could possibly want.
2. Being content with everything you have.

But maybe there's a third way, which is to learn to be content with what you have, while setting clear goals to attain, over time, the things you want.

What's so unique about your holistic approach to wealth?

While everyone else is trying to get you to buy what they're selling, I want to teach, empower, and inspire you to understand wealth principles, so you can do it yourself. For me, there are six parts to wealth:

W — Well informed, well-educated and inspired to master your money and get it working for you.

E — Engaged and empowered with your money, finances and future, to make the changes that will get you where you want to be.

A — Actively using accelerated debt reduction systems and processes (ADRs) to get debt-free as soon as possible.

L — Leveraging your income by using other people's money (OPM) and ultimately leaving a legacy for those you love.

T — Taking home more tax, while using tax-effective solutions and strategies wherever you can, to maximise every dollar you earn.

H — Holistic and happy! Money covers so many areas of your life, including your legacy, so you need to take a holistic approach that makes you happy. Whatever you're doing, if it's not making you joyful, content and fulfilled, then change it. Happiness should be the ultimate goal!

How can people start their wealth journey?

After hundreds of conversations with everyday Australians, which equates to thousands of hours of individual consulting and coaching sessions, I've come to the conclusion that there are five things Australians generally want, namely to increase their income, have more cashflow, be debt free, pay less tax and have a fantastic future to look forward to.

These are, in fact, the Five Pillars to Wealth. They're pretty easy to follow once you know how, and yet sadly are so often misunderstood, because we were never taught how to master our money.

Why do we need to learn how to master our money?

Simply put, if you don't master your money, you will become its slave. According to the Australian Bureau of Statistics, seventy-six percent of Australians retire on *less than* $20,000 a year. That's around $400 a week to try and survive on in retirement! What sort of a fantastic future do you think you'll have trying to adjust?

And it gets worse. According to Morgan Stanley, one of the world's largest investment banks, Australia's household debt is the highest, or near highest, in the world. Our debts are getting out of hand.

Financial stress is on the rise, as are divorce rates, many due to financial stress. And a sad outcome is that one in three single women over the age of sixty are living below the poverty line.

It would seem we're not doing so well. Our debts are getting out of control, our stress is increasing, our divorce rates are rising, our marriages are breaking down and our families are suffering. We're not calm; we're in a state of dis-ease. And unfortunately, stress-related disease is the outcome for an increasing number of us. These include heart disease, high blood pressure, obesity, diabetes and worse. It sometimes causes me to wonder if our obsession with debt is the great hidden 'dis-ease' behind it all.

But it's not really your fault.

When I sit down with a private client for the first time and coach them through some simple solutions and strategies, explain what's going wrong and show them how to dramatically improve their wealth with super simple and safe changes, the most frequent comment back to me is, "Dave, we just weren't taught this at school".

What would you say is your mission and passion?

Who has ever shown you, taught you or coached you, simply, methodically and strategically, how to increase your income, pay less tax, destroy your debts, own your home quicker and supercharge your super?

Probably no one!

Well, that's why my mission and passion are pretty simple: to help everyday Australians like you be debt free. I want you to live a life of choice and freedom today, and well into your future, so you can leave a legacy for those you love.

What are the three underlying principles to all aspects of wealth?

There are three timeless, underlying principles to all aspects of your wealth generation journey that *must* be applied, or at least referred to, no matter what stage you're at.

- Work hard to *earn your money*.
- Work hard to *keep your money*.
- Get your money to *work hard for you*.

- **Point One: Earn Your Money**
  If you don't earn it, you'll never have it in the first place.

  Money probably won't fall from the sky into your lap, no matter how many lotto tickets you buy or get-rich-quick videos you watch.

- **Point Two: Keep Your Money**
  If you don't keep it...well...you simply have to start all over and earn it again!

  In which case, see point one.

- **Point Three: Make Your Money Work for You**
  If all you do is keep your money, due to inflation alone, it will lose its value over time, and you'll have to go back to point one...again!

  And this is when I realised where grandpa Cliffy failed. He worked hard to earn his money, but he kept it (to some extent) hidden under the bed, without ever getting it to work for him.

  You need to get your money to work hard for you. Make it earn an income. And ideally, you'll use the second secret of the wealthy: using other people's money and the seven ways to leverage it, which are both covered in more detail in my workshops and live events.

How can this be achieved?
I've developed a proprietary, simple framework and process that I take all of my private clients and attendees to my live events through, and it starts with understanding the Five Pillars to Wealth and the Cashflow Conundrum.

The Five Pillars to Wealth
1. Increase your income.
2. Create more cash flow.
3. Destroy your debts.
4. Pay less tax.
5. Focus on a fantastic future.

With a bit of education and coaching, these five pillars are easy to follow. You just need to be shown how. So why do we tend to get it all wrong? The simple answer is this that we get stuck in a *cashflow conundrum*.

We tend to focus on one thing, and one thing only, and that is increasing our income. Now don't get me wrong. I'm all about helping people increase their income, and in fact, with many of my private clients and students, we help you develop *multiple* income streams.

But, and it's a major but, if that's all you're focused on, it can go pear-shaped pretty quickly. Let me explain.

Earning more money is great, but it can trick us into this line of thinking:

Surely if my income has gone up, I'm earning more money. And if I'm earning more money, I'll have more cash flow. And if I have more cash flow, I can get my debts under control. And if I'm paying my debts down, one day my future will be fantastic!

That sounds nice. It might make you smile. But does that actually happen?

What is the cashflow conundrum?

Let's be honest.

What tends to be the first thing that happens to us when we start earning more money?

We spend more! We buy more food, more clothes and a new phone. We purchase more shoes, more golf clubs, a bigger TV or whatever takes our fancy. We also get the bigger car, the bigger house and the bigger credit card. Our debts go up.

Let that sink in for a moment. As our income goes up, our spending goes up and our debts go up. So, what happens to our cash flow?

It very often goes down!

Income Up = Spend Up + Debts Up = Cashflow Down = ☹

Not only that, but what's the other thing that's guaranteed to go up as we earn more money?

We pay more taxes!

Your income has gone up, and you're earning more money, but maybe you're spending more, and your debts have gone up, and now you're also paying more tax!

What happens to our cash flow now?

It's possibly getting a bit tight.

And what happens to our future?

We ignore it by burying our heads in the sand like an ostrich and telling ourselves, *it doesn't matter. I've got plenty of time to sort that out later...*

And this is partly where we get it so wrong. We neglect our future for the sake of now. We've forgotten the ancient and contemporary wisdom and practise of delayed gratification, as detailed by Scott Peck in his book, *The Road Less Traveled*. We don't like to wait for what we want anymore.

What do people tend to do instead?

We tend to earn more money to pay off our debts and keep up with the lifestyle and spending we've grown accustomed to. We earn more and work harder, which adds to our stress that we then alleviate by spending more on food, alcohol, entertainment and other 'stuff' we often don't need, that we think will make us happy.

This is known as being caught in the rat race cycle.

And at this time, I'd like to make two points.

1. I don't think you're a rat.
2. Why are you in a race to start with? A race to what exactly? And with whom?

No matter how many shoes you have, you will only ever have two feet, and no matter how many golf clubs you own, you only have two hands. At some stage, you need to ask yourself, *When is enough, actually enough*?

Now, I'm not somebody who advocates eating baked beans while living like a pauper. Life is to be enjoyed...but not necessarily at the expense of robbing ourselves of an awesome future.

So how can people start to turn this around?

You just need to make a few simple changes. Get away from that vicious rat race and build a positive *cashflow cycle* that can grow and grow, and end up snowballing your financial future. This means going back to the Five Pillars to Wealth.

How can people use the Five Pillars to Wealth?

1. **Increase your Income**

    As our income increases, we want to do two things differently. First, we should direct a percentage of it towards our future. Please note that there's an ideal number, and one that in fact supercharges this for you, but just a percentage will do for now. The most critical point is that you make a change.

    At the same time, you want to think about directing some extra money to pay your debts down and eventually *destroy your debt*.

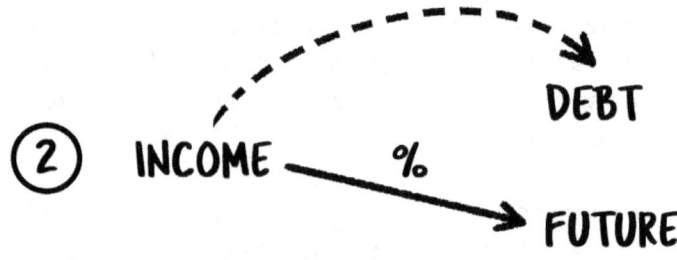

Now, let me ask you this. If you're paying down your debts, is your future getting worse or better?

It's getting better!

I'm sure you'll agree that having no debts in your future is a good thing. So, by focusing extra money there, you're also *focusing on your future*.

Debt Down = Better Future ☺

By having no debts, you have increased cash flow.

Better Future = More Cashflow ☺

2. **Create More Cashflow**

    So now we can say that by paying our debts down, our future looks brighter, and we're *creating more cashflow*.

    Debt Down = Better Future = More Cashflow ☺

    What do we do with more Cashflow?

3. **Destroy Your Debt**

    Well…as our cash flow increases, we can direct even more money to paying off our debts and making our future even more fantastic. This is where the snowball effect 'kicks in'.

    Debt Down = Better Future = More Cashflow = Debt Down = Better Future = More Cashflow = Debt Down = Better Future = More Cashflow = Debt Down ☺☺☺

    And now we've moved from a vicious rat race to building a positive cycle!

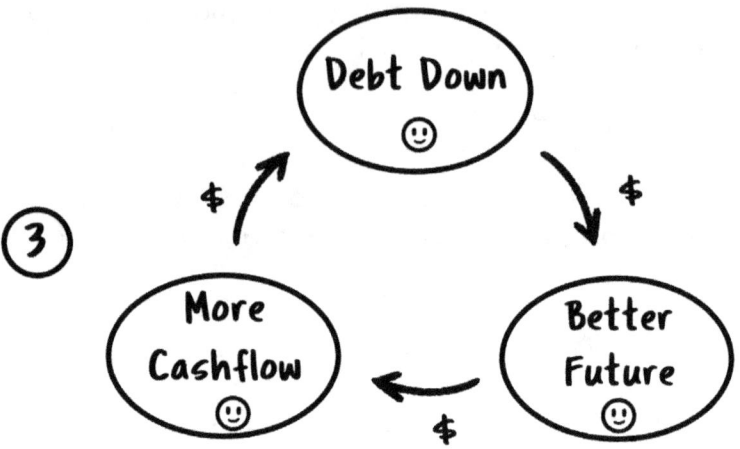

All we need to do now is…

4. **Pay Less Tax**

   So, let me ask you this. Do you think there might be ways, strategies, tips or tricks the wealthy use to not only build their wealth, but to *pay less tax* at the same time? You bet there is! And some of them are super safe, super simple and super easy.

   And in order to get to this point, we need to go back to the future. No, not the classic Michael J Fox movie, but back to what you were putting a percentage of your income into.

We need to think about putting some money towards our future by getting some

- IPAs
- CGAs
- WPAs.

What am I taking about?

Income-producing assets, capital growth assets and wealth-protecting assets. In simple terms, these are assets that increase your income and grow and protect your wealth.

Increase. Grow. Protect

Think of it like this: If you're putting money into an income-producing asset, you're *increasing your income*.

If you're also putting money aside into a capital growth asset, *you're growing your wealth*.

If you're also setting money aside for the correct wealth-protecting assets, you're *protecting your income and your wealth*.

Protecting your wealth, while ensuring you don't lose money, is pretty important.

> "The first rule of investing is, don't lose money.
> The second rule is, don't forget rule number one."
> *~Warren Buffet*

Now, the fun part to all of this is that there are ways of putting your money into income-producing assets, capital growth assets and wealth-protecting assets that also help you *pay less tax!*

You might be saying to yourself, *Huh? I can increase my income, grow my wealth, protect them both and pay less tax?*

Yes, you can. Some of these IPAs, CGAs and WPAs (when structured correctly) can also dramatically help you pay less tax!

5. **Focus on Your Future**

    An example of focusing on your future is how some well-chosen, investment-grade properties can produce income, grow in value and provide considerable tax advantages. Contributing extra money into our super grows our future wealth and gives us massive tax returns. Some WPAs that are structured well can also give us tax breaks. Now we can say that by focussing on our future, we not only increase our income, but also pay less tax.

    Income % to Future = Better Future = Pay Less Tax = Increase Cashflow = Debt Down = Better Future

    And so the cycle continues, and the snowball effect kicks into overdrive.

    This process looks like the graphic below. But if you'd like to see a better explanation presented live, head to *daveparry.com.au/fivepillars*.

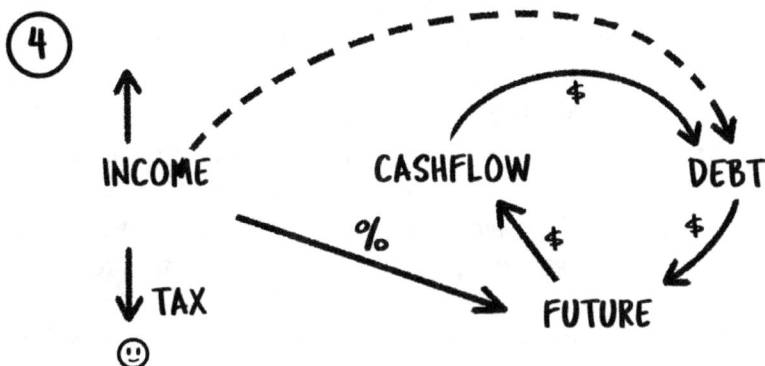

If your head is spinning a bit, or you're not quite getting it…that's pretty normal!

The idea is logical and radical at the same time, but a little hard to grasp just by reading this. At my live events, I go through it in much more detail, and this is the exact starting point I take all of my private clients through to save them thousands in tax, hundreds off their home loan and potentially help double their retirement figure.

What else can someone do to turn things around and get out of the rat race?

1. **You need a Freedom Vision.**

    My Grandpa Cliffy used to say that you can't be optimistic if you've got a misty optic! In other words, if you don't know where you're going, you could end up anywhere. So, a clear vision is vital …and ideally, you also need something to follow.

    The well-known coach, motivator and sales trainer, Brian Tracy, has often said, "Success leaves a trail". This simply means that if you can find someone who is successful, just follow what they've done, and the hard work is over. So why not follow a simple, safe and streamlined path or process that has a brilliant track record?

Do you have an exciting, clear vision of where your financial future is taking you? Are you on the fast-track to being debt-free, while supercharging your super and leaving a legacy for those that you love? Do you have a clear process to follow? Have you found the path that will get you there? Do you know the steps to take?

What's a freedom vision? It's where you see yourself tasting freedom, and for many of us that starts with being debt-free.

At my live events, attendees work out *within the first few hours* exactly what date they will start to taste freedom. As part of that process, it's common for people to save over $30,000 with just a few simple changes.

2. **You need a Freedom System.**

    Anyone and everyone who is successful, follows a system. It's as simple as that. Success leaves a trail. All you need to do is follow a tried-and-tested process.
    The freedom system saves you

    - time
    - money
    - stress.

    So, if you want more time, more money, and less stress, you need a system. And ideally, you want a simple and safe process. The system I teach and coach people through takes away your headaches. It helps you track your vision and saves money and tax. You become debt-free quickly, while on autopilot, without ever having to think about the word 'budget' ever again. A safe and simple system can streamline your life and makes finance fun. At my live events, we introduce you to the five most common systems, and you choose the one that suits you the best.

3. **You need a Freedom Strategy.**
    Having a vision is motivating. Having a system is even better. But what's your strategy? What steps are you going to put in place first? What do you need to do immediately and put time aside for to get right? What are some quick wins or simple changes you can make today that will keep you motivated and inspired? How do you know what to do first?

Some of the questions you might ask yourself are the following:

- Do I pay off my home loan, my credit card or my car loan first?
- Should I put aside money for my super or pay off my debts?
- If I boost my super, should I do it through my salary or put it in myself?
- Should I pay off my home loan quicker or invest in the stock market?
- What strategies should I use first to save on my taxes?
- Can I afford an investment property? And if so, should I pay it or my own home off first? Should an investment property be in my name or is it better to buy one in my super? Or should I use a trust or company?

Aaarrggghhhh!!! Maybe I'll go back to being an Ostrich.

If you don't have a strategy to follow, you may become overwhelmed or confused, and hesitate to take action. But action is the key. Having a sound, simple strategy makes taking action smooth and easy, thus elevating your results quickly.

4. **You need a Freedom Team.**

    If you look at the most successful people in the world, you'll see that they haven't achieved greatness on their own. Instead, they've built up a team of experts to help them accomplish one solitary goal: elevating their results.

    This incredible team is usually a mix of individuals who are experts in one specific field, working together as a team.

    You know the saying, "Too many cooks spoil the broth"? The most successful restaurants in the world don't have a kitchen full of cooks, all vying for attention and wanting to prepare different meals, prove their recipes are the best and hog the stove while making a mess. That would be a disaster.

    Instead, they have a range of people doing specific tasks to produce sensational meals over and over again in the most time and cost-effective way. They have the best kitchen hand, sous chef, saucier, plater, servers, etc.

    And ideally, they have the best master chef overseeing the entire process, constantly monitoring, coaching and making sure the dishes are produced with the same quality, over and over again.

    This concept applies to your money, finance and freedom. *You need a team* that would consist of the following:
    - a home loan expert
    - a tax expert
    - a structure expert
    - a property expert
    - a super expert
    - a shares expert
    - an insurance expert

And so on. Also, all of these experts need to be working for you on your vision, system and strategy, while helping you supercharge your finances and elevate your results.

And ultimately, instead of a master chef, you need a 'master coach', pulling this team together and keeping the focus one hundred percent on you.

Do you have any last words to share?

As one of Australia's most trusted and sought-after wealth coaches, financial educators and presenters, I've been privileged to serve and help hundreds of people completely transform their financial world.

So, where to go from here?

If any of this has resonated with you, made a few things clearer or mapped out some solid steps for you to take, I suggest you jump over and have a look at my website. See if one of my free events makes sense for you, so together, we can empower you to elevate your results.

> "Master your money, or you will become its slave.
> Prosper with property, or pay the price,
> Focus on your future, or face the consequences."
> ~ Dave Parry, Wealth Coach
> daveparry.com.au

 To discover more about how Dave can help you *Elevate Your Results*, simply visit www.elevatebooks.com/results

Angela Rettie
Fulfilling Decisions

Angela Rettie is an internationally certified results coach, investor, business owner, writer, presenter and educator.

After an early career in corporate sales and marketing, both in the UK and Australia, she's carved out her niche as a lifestyle entrepreneur, creating and selling several businesses, all while juggling being a wife and mother.

Angela blends her passion for learning and growing, along with her diverse life and business experiences, into practical, action-oriented, client-focused coaching and educating. She loves to help people break through resistance around their decisions and adapt to their own changes and challenges, so they can be free to create and enjoy a fulfilling life.

You can find more about Angela Rettie at www.angelarettie.com

Angela Rettie

Fulfilling Decisions

What decisions have you made that caused your life to change?

As you can imagine, I've made a few! We all make small decisions every day that influence our lives.

However, the big ones that get us moving and changing our course interest me the most. Usually, these decisions are heavily influenced by our ability to embrace who we really are or who we want to become.

There are two decisions that have had a significant impact on my life. One was moving to Australia, and the other was when I decided to reassess my life, which eventually led me to become a coach.

My decision to move represents the power of digging deep and finding my *do-or-die* leverage. It's about taking a leap of faith to propel myself outside of my comfort zone with total commitment. My path to becoming a coach was more of a slow burn, an evolution to discovering the next chapter of my life, where the results are still unfolding.

Both decisions are the start of a journey and demonstrate the power and importance of staying true to my authentic self.

What made you decide to move to Australia?

When I was twenty-five years old, I went on holiday to visit a friend in Western Australia. Returning to the UK on April Fool's Day, I felt like the joke was on me. The thought of going back to my busy life in crowded London just seemed crazy.

Fulfilling Decisions

After returning home, I immediately hatched a plan to get a working holiday visa and head back to Australia. The first two actions I took were to get a new passport and apply for my visa.

The next action was to book the flights. It was 1989, and there were no internet bookings, so it took a phone call to a travel agent to get this done. Everything seemed to be going well until the agent told me she had seats available on the flight, and I needed to confirm and pay for my ticket immediately. In a panic, I seized up and told her I would call her back before abruptly putting the phone down.

Until that point, all of my actions had been within my comfort zone. Every step I'd taken could be unwound with little or no consequence.

I thought I had already made the decision. I'd been taking the actions, but in my head, the one that counted the most felt irreversible. This was my do-or-die moment.

How did you make that decision?

As I stared at the telephone on my office desk, this is what I was thinking: *Okay, this is* real. *I'm either calling the travel agent back to book my flight to Sydney, or I'm going to live the rest of my life in England. If I stay, I'll work at this office and rise up through the ranks of my job. I'll have expensive clothes and be paid really well. I'll have a house in London, eventually buy myself a yacht and a flat in Brighton, and I'll drive down each weekend in my Porsche 911.*

To many people, the second option would sound like living the dream. To me, the idea felt like a slow death. A resignation to, as Henry David Thoreau wrote, leading a life of quiet desperation. Even now, as I look back and remember the thoughts that flashed through my head, the picture is all dark grey and black.

Angela Rettie

> "Open your eyes, look within. Are you satisfied with the life you are living?"
> ~ *Bob Marley*

I had the realisation that I was living my life in the shadows of other people's expectations. Study hard, go to university, get a degree and get a good job—all well-meaning expectations. But I wasn't happy where I was, nor where I could see myself heading.

And there it was, in a flash—the pain point, the leverage, the emotion. The agony of staying and not living true to myself was too much for me to bear.

I've always been someone who makes the most of pretty much any situation, which can be a blessing and a curse. When you do this, sometimes you can trap yourself. You settle. And I'd been settling.

Deep down, I knew there was more to life for me. I needed to see what else I could do to break free. I had to prove it to myself. Until that point, I felt like I'd been attached to imaginary elastic bungee cords that gave me a little room for movement, but not too much. They were holding me in place, keeping me comfortable in my current life.

Imagining the future pain of knowing I'd played it safe and that I'd allowed the invisible force of other people's expectations to hold me back was so sharp and real, I pulled on those bungees hard and fast. And when they broke, I was catapulted way outside of my comfort zone. Looking back, I realised that was the moment the real decision was made.

I immediately picked up the phone to book the flight.

And the rest, as they say, is history. That was August. I resigned from my job and left in September. By the end of October, I was on a plane from London to Toronto. I spent three weeks in Canada travelling overland by train on my own. Then I flew from Vancouver to Sydney, Australia, arriving on Tuesday, 21st November 1989.

By Thursday that week, I had a job with a company that ended up sponsoring me into Australia. By the weekend, I'd moved into a three-storey house overlooking Watson's Bay Park, and the people I moved in with became my surrogate family.

Less than two months later, I met Andrew. Two and a half years later, we married and have now been together for over twenty-eight years.

> "...that the moment one definitely commits oneself,
> then Providence moves, too."
> ~ *William H. Murray*

What made you decide on a career in coaching?

It was July 2016. I was fifty-one years old.

I was standing in the middle of the busy concourse of Dubai Airport early one morning, heading from Australia to London, UK, and feeling overwhelmed.

Why would the same woman who'd left all the comforts of a good job, friends, and family to relocate by herself halfway around the world, be feeling overwhelmed?

I realised this was the first time in more than twenty years that I'd travelled solo internationally. I had to ask myself if I was just out of practice, or if it was something more.

Angela Rettie

First, the reason I never travelled alone during those years was that I'd become a mother. I'd also left my corporate job, started businesses, and relocated states from NSW to Victoria, and then to Queensland. We moved houses many times, rarely staying in one place for more than two years at a time. We experienced the highs and lows, from earning a high-income to living off our investments, eventually getting into debt, and finally landing back on our feet.

With two teenage children still at home, I needed a break before I could even consider what I'd do next in my life. Everything seemed like a struggle, and I didn't feel I had the energy to do more than I was.

I'd been creating online businesses with some success, but the initial thrill had gone. I'd proved I could do it, but there was no feeling that I'd accomplished something truly fulfilling, and when I looked forward in my life, I knew it wasn't where I wanted to go.

I felt so stuck in my life, like I was in a holding pattern. I was emotionally exhausted and unhappy with putting everything off to the future when I had more money, energy or time. I felt like a shell of a woman, empty inside.

I only spent the money to travel this time, because I'd just learned that my father had been diagnosed with stage 4 cancer, so it might be the last time I would have a chance to spend time with my parents and all of my siblings together.

As I stood in that massive airport, surrounded by the buzz of people from all around the world, I realised I'd been focussing on me and my little bubble of life in Brisbane. I'd been putting off my 'decisions' to make any changes for a better future until everything lined up and was perfect.

'Until' was a timeframe that was constantly slipping out of my grasp, and 'perfect' was an impossible standard that could bring no joy. If I didn't change and adapt, I was going to have regrets for all I could have done but didn't. This was an evolution. An adapt-or-die moment.

I wondered where that courageous twenty-five-year-old me, with the faith, joy and love of life, had gone. And then I realised it was *still* me. I just had to give myself permission to live life authentically on my terms, starting right now.

I felt so connected to something magical in the Dubai Airport that morning. Even though I don't know what it was, I'm so grateful for it. I went from overwhelmed to energised. My eyes opened wide, and I became filled with a sense of hope and possibility.

I didn't know exactly what I was going to do, but I knew deep down in my heart I'd find something that would make me happy and fulfilled. I needed to start putting myself first. To work on my mindset and my energy, and get back to enjoying life in the moment.

This decision was different from the breaking of the bungees. That had been the external forces of other people's expectations, keeping me back. This one was more like a sharp slap across the face to wake myself up and take control of my own life once again or live with the regret that I could have done and been more.

My first action towards this decision probably seems a bit strange, but it was a turning point. I arrived in the UK fully aware, taking everything in with the biggest smile on my face. I decided to find all of the love and connection with everything, not just my family, and fall back in love with the UK. Even though the circumstances were quite challenging and sad, I remember it as a time full of joy and laughter while making the most of the precious time we had.

> "Many people die with their music still in them. Why is this so? Too often, it is because they are always getting ready to live. Before they know it, time runs out."
> ~ *Oliver Wendell Holmes Snr*

Why is mindset so important?

Mindset is critical, and it comes *first*!

When your mindset is aligned and free, it's easier to make good decisions and take action towards them. There's much less resistance and more chance of success.

Your confidence is up. Your energy is up. You have clarity, and you're resourceful and adaptable. You're open to change and evolve as you go. You know you'll find a way to clear away the obstacles and handle fears or uncertainties.

Mindset is what gets you moving and keeps you moving forward. Most people focus on the skills, not the mindset, but they're doing themselves a disservice. Very few people start new projects, businesses or even new lifestyle habits, focusing on mindset, let alone thinking about investing in it.

> "Success in business and life is eighty per cent psychology and twenty per cent mechanics."
> ~ Tony Robbins

How did you figure out what you wanted to do in life?

After my wakeup call, I got back home to Australia in late August 2016 and knew it was essential to get myself back into a better frame of mind. And I also needed to rediscover the creativity and resourcefulness I'd had in my younger days.

While I'd studied many personal development books, tapes, videos and courses, I'd barely touched them since the mid-1990s. So, the first thing I did was take stock of them and start re-reading and studying what I thought would be relevant.

A few weeks later, I saw an offer for Tony Robbins' Unleash the Power Within event in Sydney for 2017. I immediately booked two tickets, and that was the start of my immersive personal development journey.

Since then, I've invested significant time, energy and money into my personal growth and mindset.

What contributed the most to your success?

The better question to ask is, "If you knew about investing in mindset in the 1990s, why didn't you keep on track in your life?"

Good question—embarrassing answer!

Learning was only part of the equation. And while I did have success, I'd still lost my way for a long time. What got me back on track was having a coach.

If you're not sure if your mindset is on track, many coaches offer discovery calls. It's like getting a check-up or assessment from someone who can see what you might not be able to recognise in yourself.

I've had my coach for a couple of years. She's helped me define and refine what I want and shows me my blind spots. She helps me be accountable to myself and enables me to move forward, faster and further than I'd thought possible.

Like I once did, many people think they're pretty smart and don't need a coach. But when you have a good one you really connect with, you'll see the shortcuts you can take, and you'll never want to go back.

Angela Rettie

There are so many ways my coach helps me. We discuss my plans, what to do next and how to keep me focused on what's most important. At times she's a sounding board, a resource, and my buddy to celebrate with. She brings to the table her wealth of skills in business and her studied disciplines. She challenges my thinking and asks thought-provoking questions. I've embraced areas of my life I didn't think I could or would, and have started to really grow and shine. We love to outdo each other on the resources we share with each other, and we've been known to have a dance-off on the phone.

Coaching helped me through one of the most difficult periods in my life when both of my parents passed away within four months of each other. Without it, I would never have had the courage to give the eulogy at my mother's funeral.

Having a coach helps me be even more effective for my clients. I know what it's like to be new to coaching, not knowing what to do or what to expect. I understand the fears and apprehension of coming to the first session, and I've learned what it takes to transition from being new to coaching to getting real value out of it.

Until I had my own coach, I thought they were an extravagance. In contrast, I now see it as a necessity and an investment in myself and my future.

What was your biggest life lesson?

Since 2016, when I received the news of my father's terminal cancer, and then in 2018, with my mother getting a similar diagnosis, I've realised that you never know how much time you have. You can get more money, but you can't get more time.

Therefore, I would say my biggest life lesson is finding ways to maximise and spend my time wisely.

The main goal of most people, in some form or another, is to create financial freedom. But I don't believe it's about the money. I think we create wealth, so we can have the time to do the things we really want.

The quality of your life is determined by what you decide to spend your time doing and who you choose to spend your time with.

What do you do to make the most of your time?

Becoming aware of what matters most to you is vital. Once you know this, it's so much easier to decide what you'll spend your time on and who you will spend it with.

Do you know where you're spending your time? Is it on the important stuff? Where could you shift things around?

I love learning and working on my mindset. They're both high priorities for me. I can listen to courses, audiobooks or podcasts while doing other activities like driving my car or walking the dog, so I'm more efficient with my time. But while that's a specific, tangible outcome, I knew there were other ways to make the most of my time, like reframing my attitude to any situation. For example, when my daughter was younger and was swim training twice a day, I spent a long time in the car.

When she was learning to drive, she would take us there and back, and for some reason, that made me feel like I wasn't using my time well. However, I needed to look at it with a fresh pair of eyes and see beyond the chore. I asked myself, *What can I do to reframe this task to make it even more valuable and fulfilling?*

The answer I received was that this was precious time with my daughter, just the two of us. We could talk about what was happening in her life and anything that was important to her. And as soon as she passed her test, she would no longer need me to be there.

I started focussing on what I was gaining from it rather than what I was missing out on. Changing perspective showed me that these car trips were a gift, providing both of us with a time for connection and love.

Why do some people do all they can, while others don't live up to their full potential?

I study personal development courses and read autobiographies of successful people to look for answers to these questions.

From my research, it has to do with the words *could*, *should* and *must*. For instance:

- What *could* you do?
- What *should* you do?
- What *must* you do?

Which one has the power to make you move?

- I *could* get in shape.
- I *should* get in shape.
- I *must* get in shape.

It's all about finding your deepest, most important, and compelling reason to adapt and change. Uncovering what's important, and why, is the key to breaking your invisible bungee cords or experiencing the imaginary sharp slap across your face.

When your goal is a must, it creates energy to break through, so you can make decisions, take action and live your life on your terms.

What's the biggest mistake people make?

I think the biggest mistake people make is assuming that 'making the decision' is the most important part, when in truth, it's just the beginning.

Fulfilling Decisions

The point of a decision is to get, do or become something. It's only successful when you attain your desired outcome. And that requires consistent action-taking.

It can be appealing to believe you've decided something. It seems like progress, which gives you a feeling of happiness. It's a reward. Humans love these incentives, and it's a super-easy way to congratulate yourself just for making that decision.

But you only have to look at people who make New Year's resolutions. Less than a quarter of the people keep them up by the end of January, and less than ten per cent accomplish what they set out to do. In the end, you feel like there's no point in making decisions anymore because you know you won't follow through.

It's easy to start believing that you aren't good at making decisions or that you aren't, nor can you ever be, successful. This is a belief cycle that can quickly spiral downwards. Repeated frustration can create stress, and then you stop making any decisions. That's where you get stuck. That's where I got stuck.

Why do you think people stay stuck?

I believe it's a fear of change that keeps people stuck.

Change is inevitable, because you never really stay still. If you do nothing, you deteriorate or go backwards. It's a law of nature.

Amongst my clients, some know exactly what they want, and some don't. At the start, there's only one difference between these two: one is ready for change, and the other is fearful of it.

When I hear people say they don't know what they want in life, I remember what it felt like to be in their position. When I didn't know what I wanted, I could barely imagine what was possible, because deep down, I was scared of what the changes would mean to my family and to me. I was also afraid of being successful and of failure. When I look back, it seems obvious, but at the time, I had no idea these dual and opposing fears existed.

Many things can hold us back, such as old beliefs, emotions from previous experiences or conflicts.

The real reason some people struggle to get on with what they really want in life is not that they don't know, but that they're afraid of change, so they resist it.

How do you help your clients move forward?

Everyone's journey is different, and that's why I believe one-on-one coaching is so valuable in helping people adapt and achieve their goals.

When I'm coaching, I work with each individual at their pace to help them achieve what they want, step by step. We don't always rigidly follow a sequence, one after the other. It depends on the client and where they are. We can spend more time in one area than another, and we loop back as needed.

Here are some of the essential elements of my program:

- **Set Yourself Up for Success**

    To make good decisions, you need to be free to make them. Your mind has to be clear, open and resourceful.

    If you're feeling stuck and can't make the decisions you know you need to for your future, try something different. It can be as simple as getting your body moving or taking a break away from your everyday life to clear your head.

- **Find Your Fuel Source**

    Find and tap into the energy source that will get you moving and keep you moving towards what you want, even when things don't go your way or get tough. What is this energy source? It's often your *Why*. Ask yourself, *Why is this important to me?'*

    Dig until you discover the energy already within you, so you can break those bungee cords and catapult yourself towards your commitment to follow through. Life-changing decisions require the most fuel or energy.

    You may already be aware of what's important to you and why, but dig deep here. You may well be surprised by what you find.

    If you still need some more energy to get you moving, ask yourself questions about what the consequences will be if you don't figure out and strive for what's important to you, such as:

    - How will my life be?
    - Who will I become?
    - Who won't I become?
    - What will I feel?
    - What won't I feel?
    - What regrets will I have if I don't make the changes?
    - What happens if I delay or wait?

    Find the emotional fuel to get you moving and keep you moving towards your outcome.

- **Specify Your Desired Outcome**

    This is where you get to design your life and imagine what it would be like to achieve what you want and become the person you've always wanted to be. The more vividly you can describe it, the more power you will find in moving towards it.

Don't know what you want? Then borrow this goal to start with: *Find out what I can do.*

Setting a goal to *find out* is one of the most powerful decisions you can make.

> "You may not be able to do all you find out, but make sure you find out all you can do."
> ~ E. James Rohn

- **Uncover Your Saboteurs**

    You've found out what you want and why you want it, but you still wonder if you can have, do or become it. Now it's time to uncover what might undo your decision. It doesn't matter where the sabotage comes from, internally or externally.

    These saboteurs will test your resolve and discover if you will do *whatever it takes* to push through. They're like those invisible bungees still attached or trying to reattach.

    The internal ones can be deeply buried beliefs, past experiences or conflicts. The external ones could be all of the 'opportunities' that might be better than the one you've picked, or another skill you feel you need to learn before you can do what you want.

    The worst saboteurs allow you to think you're making progress towards what you want, when in reality, you aren't.

    Do you know all of your saboteurs? You may only be aware of a few. Look in the mirror and be honest with yourself.

Fulfilling Decisions

- **Prepare Yourself**

    You need to figure out what you already have and what you need to start moving forward. You've got the right attitude, fuel and energy to put in the effort, and now it's time to create a plan of action. Ask yourself questions like:

    - What do I already have?
    - What do I need?
    - Who can I learn from?
    - Who can help me?
    - What steps should I take, and what order should I take them in?

    The plan is your roadmap to your destination.

- **Take Action**

    Taking action is a sneaky one because everything you've been doing to get to this point *is* taking action. You're already moving forward, so now it's all about what actions will keep you moving in the right direction.

- **Create A Feedback System**

    Your journey won't be in a straight line. Just like in a game of snakes and ladders, there may be detours along the way, and you'll discover short cuts.

    But unlike snakes and ladders, you aren't relying on the roll of the dice. You get to learn from those who know the area better than you do. In the same way, you can get distracted and off track. That's why a feedback system is critical to keep you moving in the right direction.

One of the best feedback systems is to have a regular check-in with someone who will keep you accountable.

What do you think is your life purpose?

As I mentioned earlier, I believe time is the most precious commodity that cannot be recovered once it's spent. One of the greatest tragedies for a human being is to look back on their life with regret at what they haven't done and realise they don't have the time to change it or make amends.

I've come to understand the value of creating a happy, fulfilling life without regrets. I believe my life's purpose is to use my gifts of learning, teaching and coaching to help others discover and create their compelling life story.

Through my writing, presenting, and one-on-one coaching, I help people uncover and break through the resistance around their decisions, so they can be free to create and live a happy and fulfilling life while enjoying their incredible journey.

~ **Time to Decide** ~

"If you don't know what you want in life, decide right now to focus ALL of your efforts on finding out, as if your life depended on it—because it does."
~ Angela Rettie

To discover more about how Angela can help you *Elevate Your Results*, simply visit www.elevatebooks.com/results

Chele Tindall
Empowered Results

Chele Tindall is an international speaker, teacher and author. She enables people to shift the conditioned behaviours that keep them locked in by raising their awareness.

Chele has educated and empowered people around the world to elevate their mindset through the sharing of ideas and principles. She teaches that we're all subject to the laws of the universe, and how we can all benefit from them once we understand and learn how to work with them. Chele's study and application of these key principles has allowed her to create a global business.

Chele cares deeply about affecting change and finds immense joy in knowing the ripple effect that flows when a genuine transformation has been achieved.

Chele Tindall

Empowered Results

What drives you?

Freedom.
Being free to be me!

I'm driven to work collaboratively with people who are seeking to become more in life and help them find opportunities that offer advancement in their career path, without imposed glass ceilings or stifling of their growth and well-being.

I'm driven by innovative processes that enhance how we 'do what we've always done' in a simplified, effective, more efficient way, while generating leveraged results.

This poem by James T. Moore eloquently sums up my thoughts with regard to my drive, the commitment I have to maintaining an individual's uniqueness and their freedom to live truthfully and fully.

One and Only You
Every single blade of grass,
And every flake of snow
Is just a wee bit different
There's no two alike, you know.

From something small, like grains of sand,
To each gigantic star
All were made with this in mind:
To be just what they are!
How foolish then, to imitate-

How useless to pretend!
Since each of us comes from a mind
Whose ideas never end.

There'll only be just one of me
To show what I can do
And you should likewise feel very proud
There's only ONE of YOU.

That is where it all starts
With you, a wonderful
Unlimited human being.

If you were speaking to your younger self, what advice would you give?

I would say, "Relax and enjoy the unfolding of your life. Show up with beauty and grace, knowing everything is in perfect order and operates by law".

I would also tell her, "It's important to make your own way in life based on knowing what's best for you. Don't allow other people to have influence over you or dictate what they think is right for you".

I would also tell her to live by the last two lines of William Earnest Henry's poem, *Invictus*:

I am the master of my fate; I am the captain of my soul.

I would say, "Use this mantra as a reminder to go after what you want. Be true to your inner compass, and follow what's most important to you. Don't let other people take control of your life. You only have one chance to live it the best you can...so, to your own self be true".

And finally, I would tell her, "Leave everyone you meet with an impression of increase. Your genuine and uplifting gestures, smile and words can light up someone's world. Understand that your impression has the ability to create an ever-lasting effect by leaving someone feeling better after being in contact with you".

How would you like to be remembered?

As someone who inspired others to live their life in a more fulfilling way and was a shining example for my boys, my family, and those who knew me well. And for having the courage to 'raise the bar'.

I will expand and explain what I mean, by sharing my historical and personal perspective.

It became obvious to me that throughout my entire entrepreneurial journey, I encountered a 'conflicting force' more than once, which resulted in outcomes that were NOT conducive to enhancing the bottom-line of my business or my long-term performance.

Naively, in my earlier days in business, I took people at their spoken word, with full expectation their declaration would be their bond! I believed what a colleague said about a collaborative approach on a project, especially in regard to the desired result, including the betterment and rewards for all people involved.

Little did I realise at this point in time, that their underlying intentions and actions were purposefully orchestrated to undermine and manipulate the process. And as a consequence, the process became completely destructive, to the detriment of delivering on the proposed outcome. Lesson learned. Know people by their actions, not their words.

> "When someone shows you who they are,
> believe them the first time."
> ~ Maya Angelou

This incident certainly balanced my inflated view of life that everyone has good intentions and led me to become more aware of the effects and consequences of operating within organisational 'cult-ure' and leadership styles.

It's said that all conflicts fall into two categories: internal and external. Internal conflict is when a character struggles with their own opposing desires or beliefs. It happens within them, and it drives their development as a character. External conflict, which I'd like to delve into further, sets a character against something or someone beyond their control.

Conflicts within an organisation can cause members to become frustrated if they feel there's no solution in sight, or their opinions are going unrecognised by other group members.

As a result, people become stressed, which adversely affects their professional and personal lives. (Ref:_www.smallbusiness.chron.com)

Why do conflicts arise in an organisation?

They can be caused by task interdependencies, status inconsistencies, jurisdictional ambiguities, communication problems, dependence on common resource pools, a lack of common performance standards and individual differences. (Ref: www.opentextbc.ca)

The bottom-line impact of unresolved conflicts in the workplace usually aren't obvious at the time it's occurring. Common outcomes of lingering, unresolved conflicts include delayed or missed deadlines, work recycling, lowered productivity and morale, increased employee turnover and sometimes even litigation. (Ref: www.tercorpartners.com)

Early warning signs of conflict, according to the National Centre for Diversity, are the following:

- Body language
- Behavioural changes
- Development of cliques
- Strange comments that puzzle you at first, until it all makes sense
- The words people choose
- People taking sides or ganging up in meetings, in the office and in the workplace
- Sickness levels creeping up.

Unresolved conflicts can also have a negative impact on the leader-employee relationship. For example, it can result in eroded trust, decreased motivation, lowered morale, increased stress and health risks, decreased performance and productivity, increased absenteeism and presenteeism (employees coming into work when they shouldn't) and increased resignations. (Ref:www.theglobalmail.com)

Many of you will relate to this firsthand through working within an organisational culture that is laden with these conflicts.

For me personally, I began to understand that the 'opposing forces' I encountered were a learning journey in themselves.

This situation is an absolute detriment to employees, as well as a business's bottom line, all for the sake of inflated egos, and a leadership style rife with manipulation and control. And then, of course, there's a takeover of the business through a persuasive power-play.

Knowing that their end game is control and victory at any cost, regardless of who's been stepped on or squashed in the process, I was fascinated and enlightened by Robert Greene's book *The 48 Laws of Power*, where I learned about identifying this behaviour as toxic narcissism.

This was a blinding insight for me and raised my awareness. It gave me the ability to grasp what I'd experienced personally in my business life. Comprehension and understanding followed in due course.

I became motivated by Robert Greene's incredible work, which helped me gain a deeper understanding of the integration of our darker side, commonly referred to as our shadow values, in a healthy and productive capacity for my own benefit and well-being.

I discovered that toxic narcissism is a reality whereby people who rate high on the scale of this spectrum, feast on controlling others.

Carl Jung says, "Everything that irritates us about others can lead us to an understanding of ourselves". He also states that "One does not become enlightened by imagining figures of light, but by making the darkness conscious".

Dr John Demartini, a well-known human behaviour specialist and leadership and performance expert, teaches that it's important to compare our actions to our *own* highest values. Our desire to be loved for who we are is achieved when we're poised and centred, in a state of balance, thus allowing our authentic, true self-worth to be expressed.

Understand that our perfectionism relies on our ability to integrate and embrace both sides. I aspire to be remembered for raising the bar and being poised, centred and balanced.

So, let's balance the bar to raise it!

What would you like your legacy to be?

I'd like to be a transformational ripple, by effecting change in a positive way.

I want to have an impact on others through education and empowerment. By teaching principles that ignite authentic leadership and understanding through raised awareness, which ushers in a genuine freedom as the global new reality.

My legacy will embrace the life-changing learnings I've embodied and taught to other people who've gone on to create a better life for themselves and are the ripple effect in their communities. Knowing I will live on through the generations, as these people continue to share this knowledge, is indeed heart-warming.

The beauty of education and teaching people how to behave in a conscious way, experiencing the joy of allowing their significance to shine brightly, is a privilege and an honour I will happily breathe life into.

What is the one message you wish to share with the world?

My main message I keep coming back to is, *Don't die with the music still inside of you*.

Sometimes we allow ourselves to be pulled off-track, never being dedicated to following the true path of what we want in life. We grant others the power to steer us towards what they think is best for us, which results in becoming too scared to step out and pursue what we desire deep-down.

I feel my emotions rise when I think about this, because it's not only the death of a person, it's the death of all the dreams they never lived, the experiences they never had, the places they never saw and the quality time not spent with loved ones, because instead they were living someone else's dream.

To me, the saddest thing is seeing all of the possibilities cast aside, because they were too afraid to go after what they really wanted, so instead they settled, choosing to pass up on all of their cherished dreams.

I really do believe I'm here to encourage others by putting the wind in people's wings, so they can embrace doing what they love, while clarifying what they're here to do and fulfilling their personal mission and vision. I want to ensure that more people don't pass over without their music expressed, so we don't wind up being deprived of the richness of their melody.

What is the worst thing that has ever happened to you, and how did you overcome it?

It was back in 2009.

For fifteen years, I was a loyal and dedicated leader of a health and wellness company. I had received their most prestigious award as their top producer for several consecutive years, which was based on business growth and overall high- performing results.

But then the large, residual income I'd worked so long and hard to build up with the laser-focus and dedication required to develop a global business to this level, was abruptly severed by the managing director.

The owners were actually selling off the assets of the company and devaluing the efficacy of the products by altering the long-standing-mission they were founded on and renowned for. The independent business partners involved were either unaware of this or chose not to speak up.

As I was travelling internationally and keeping my eye on the ball, it was clear to me what was happening. But when I aired my awareness of this change with leaders who weren't fully aware of what was going on 'behind the scenes', you might say that in hindsight, it did not serve me.

To be honest, having to deal with this event took the wind out of my sails. It was an instant train wreck. The view through a financial lens would be one perspective. However, the real pain was felt at a much deeper level, with emotional wounding through the added defamation that was orchestrated against me.

It absolutely required massive intestinal fortitude to stop feeling sorry for myself. I needed to commence the deep-dive into finding the benefits of this event, so I could begin my journey forward and clarify any philosophical 'silver linings' that could be derived.

This choice to change my attitude and mindset regarding my current reality, gave birth to my phoenix rising, a term I absolutely relate to now and is significant with regard to my renewal process.

When we choose to reframe the situation and look for the wisdom within the experience, we create a space where we're able to take control of our thoughts and direct our thinking forward. We 'build an image' for the life we desire, which in turn disrupts the pattern of 'thinking in reverse' and focusing only on the current reality of the situation.

Dr Maya Angelou says, "Nothing can dim the light which shines within".

I truly loved training, developing and inspiring top-performing leaders, and no one could steal this gift from me. The words once said to be inscribed at the Temple of Apollo at Delphi were *Know thyself*. I believe when we begin to understand and know thy *true* self, our moral compass will be the magnet that guides us in our truth and seeing the perfect path.

In life, it's ten percent what happens to you and ninety percent how you respond.

But at the time of a traumatic event, this is not what we like to hear! The truth is, I would not have been able to continue doing what I was so passionate about after the goal posts had forever been altered. To act as if nothing had changed did not sit well with me, and with a deep knowing, I was aware that this was no longer my aligned path. It would have been a far greater price for me to pay, knowing what I was partaking in.

Napoleon Hill says, "Every adversity, every failure, every heartache, carries with it the seed of an equal or greater benefit". He also says that "definiteness of decision always requires courage".

For me, deciding to stop focusing my attention on the door that had abruptly slammed shut and summon every ounce of my will to focus on a new door of opportunity, now fills me with deep gratitude and appreciation for who I am. Ultimately, the joy of expressing my unique gifts once again, without a doubt, led to the unfolding of this seed of an equivalent benefit. Success flowed once more, only this time from a more sustainable source.

Have you had any aha moments that changed everything for you?

Yes. Absolutely!

In 1998, I was fortunate enough to be travelling with a group of people on a bus from Adelaide to Queensland and got to view Bob Proctor's *You Were Born Rich* program on VHS videos. I know that my life was changed by that information, in that very moment.

Chele Tindall

I was fascinated with what I was learning, so much so that from this defining moment, I went on to develop an even greater understanding of this program by training as a certificated facilitator. The fact that I totally immersed myself into these thought-provoking lessons was a reflection of their impact on me.

However, to clarify my aha moment, the program really showed me how the mind works and how we operate simultaneously on three separate planes of being: spiritual, intellectual and physical.

With various other elements, this concept really highlighted why it is we don't do what we desire and end up doing what we dislike. For me, it was learning that I had the ability to control my thoughts, and through a creative process, it would become the starting point for all I aspired to be.

This was something I wasn't taught in school. It was so profound, knowing that we can choose and control our thoughts and direct them in a specific way to bring us whatever we're in harmony with through the Law of Vibration. Obviously, later on this became the phenomenon known as the Law of Attraction, a theory at the heart of the global sensation book and movie, *The Secret*.

This new awareness that I had the ability to choose, got me highly enthusiastic about how I could definitely create whatever I wanted in my life. My newfound knowledge to set goals through utilising and tapping into my higher faculties, enhanced the setting and attaining of my goals.

It spoke to me so deeply. I felt empowered with the level of information, the synchronicity of this material, that I came to learn at this particular time. It was awe-inspiring and incredibly timely.

My husband, three sons and those closest to me, must have felt my passion flowing freely. I was highly excited to share this knowledge.

There has been a ripple effect from just this one simple concept of knowing we've all been gifted with a will and the freedom to exercise it to create anything we want in our life. How wonderful is that?

What decisions have made a difference in your life?

Well, a huge turning point came when I chose to leave a job working in my family business. I was abandoning the safety and status quo of the familiar, to brave the unknown, new world of being an entrepreneur, pursuing my vision and the possibilities for my life. I still remember that day like it was yesterday, when my husband and I trekked off with the kids and a few belongings, and headed off to follow a dream.

The difference was life-changing! My world expanded greatly.

It brought the richness of travelling and training on a global stage into my reality. Rubbing shoulders and meeting incredible speakers and business leaders on an international platform certainly enriched not only my life, but my family's as well.

I look back on this moment and know it was monumental. I chose to be 'the master of my fate and the captain of my soul'. I was thrilled to commence this expansive journey as an entrepreneur, learning firsthand what was required to close the gap from where I was, to where I wanted to be, while earning my success in business and in life.

Realising there was no ceiling, only what was self-imposed, I became aware that I had the potential to keep growing with this process. Through service and bringing my best into everything I did, a significance flowed that allowed me to impact more lives, while reaping the rewards.

It definitely was a turning point and makes me smile as I think about the rich experience my family and I received by stepping outside of our comfort zone. We got to experience many of the rich tapestries that life could offer when we were brave enough to follow our hearts. That was a defining moment for sure.

What is the best thing that's ever happened to you, and why?

Without a doubt, the best, most uplifting and joyful moment in my life, was welcoming my three sons into the world. They have been my greatest achievement and continue to be my reason why.

I love to create a better version of myself, and they ignite that side of me where I want to do better. I've ventured outside of my comfort zone, setting an example of someone who will go beyond her limitations. I've stepped up to build an international business while travelling to many countries, so consequently, our awareness and experiences as a family increased significantly.

I now delight in seeing them as grown men, attracting their beautiful partners. It certainly has been a major highlight in my life, and I'm so fortunate to be the mother of three incredible souls who have definitely made everything better. My husband and I could not be prouder of the boys we've raised.

What are you passionate about?

I'm passionate about teaching people to live their best life. I get totally 'jived' when I see someone doing well and finding their success while unleashing their authentic self. I'm passionate about self-development.

There's something I call the 'light and joyful dance of the soul', harmoniously moving to the rhythm of our unique calling, by doing what most lights us up. It's about remaining unafraid of being whatever it is we're called to be. This allows us to have the enthusiasm and vibrancy to get up in the morning and create in a way that reflects our authentic expression of the passion within. It's about being fully expressed through the way we live our significance each and every day.

I'm passionate about seeing people thrive, not merely survive. Witnessing them express the authentic side of themselves, the pureness of their light radiating from them, it's hard not to feel inspired and immediately know this is an alive human being. It's magnetic.

I'm passionate about people finding their truth and living with joy and freedom every day. I don't want to see them getting to the end of their life with their music still inside of them, filled with regret and sadness for what could have been.

It's my calling to be a teacher and thought leader, empowering others.

What do you think are people's biggest problems in life?

One problem that I'm familiar with is people being locked into a comfort zone, too afraid of changing their situation or whatever it is that keeps them stuck. It could be they don't have the knowledge or know-how to step outside of this invisible zone and are unable to make the necessary changes. Therefore, they continue to live a 'settled-for' lifestyle and inadvertently give up on any dreams they once held for their life.

They say that being in a rut is like digging your own grave. Refusing to go after what you truly desire might be caused by not wanting to attract undue attention for fear of evoking the criticism from peers or those closest to you.

Making any change to begin improving your life does invite feedback from people around you, even though you may not have requested it. Others may not be as ecstatic as you are with your progress and are unwilling to acknowledge this change as a positive step. Adopting these uncalled-for opinions, or taking them to heart, can be the undoing of any further progress. You'll decide it's too hard and too painful. You'll crawl back inside of your shell and remain there forever, knowing you will never risk sticking your neck out ever again, for fear that next time, it could get chopped off completely!

Another problem I see is the worry and doubt that coexists when going after what you want, because of the emphasis and energy on failure and not intention. By channelling all of your energy towards the goal through the creative process, your outcome may well be your finest ever. Stepping through this doorway, and not retreating back to the safety of bondage, is such a fabulous confidence builder.

What's the best way to help them with this problem?

I believe the best path is through education and gaining a new level of understanding as you raise your conscious awareness. The ability to see and do what you previously were unable to.

At the place where you're stuck, you require someone who's capable of guiding your next steps, which will result in closing the giant gap of where you currently are, to where you desire to be. I believe having the right mentor or coach can provide a direct path to keep you on course, and more importantly, stay the course.

For me, deciding to change the problem I was experiencing was the beginning of my personal development journey of over thirty years ago now. I'm grateful for the mentors who've gone before me and were willing to share their knowledge.

In my experience, good teachers and mentors certainly know how to simplify the process, ensuring success is inevitable. By building on each small action step as you continue to develop your level of skill, the compounding effect kicks in, and you become aware of the momentum you've created. With continued focus and commitment, you will experience mastery at a world-class level.

One process that provided the most effective catalyst for me to make the necessary changes in my life, was learning how to build a new self-image. I began seeing myself as a successful businessperson, training on a global platform. At this time, it was a far-off vision from my current reality. The steps required for creating this new image was one of the most valuable lessons I learned, and I now love being able to pass on this knowledge.

Not fully embracing the entire process will draw you right back to your default self, where your existing self-image is programmed. This is an important piece of the puzzle in knowing how to create the desired future-version of yourself. By doing so, you will realise a completely new level of success and results based on this new self-image you're bringing to life.

I love seeing the change in people who've gone through this program with me, and how they embrace this concept to create their new reality. There really is no limit. It's delightful watching their problems dissolve and a new horizon open up for them. It can be achieved in a dedicated and focused, yet effortless way, through *keeping the main thing the main thing*.

I find this is one of the very best ways I can teach people and help them with a worthwhile solution that's not just a two-minute fix. This internal change is critical if you want to experience success long-term. It's a really fun process, and I encourage you to allow it to enhance your life.

Why is mindset important?

I actually think it's critical. I've heard it said that success is ninety-five percent mindset and five percent strategy. I would go along with this line of thinking.

I've trained myself, as well as other entrepreneurs over the years, in the ways of creating a winning mindset. It commands an attitude that brings a heightened level of execution and allows the strategy to flow with effortless precision.

Does visualisation help in life?

I absolutely believe it's a tremendous help.

Imagination is one of our higher faculties. Being able to evoke imagination through a visioneering process is powerful and is the way everything in life is created.

How many studies have we heard of about elite athletes who've included mental rehearsal into their preparation? Those statistics clearly reflect the power of mental rehearsal and visualisation as an important factor in achieving success.

I understand that visualisation is the creativity that helps bring thoughts into form.

Should everyone practice meditation or mindfulness?

Yes! Yes! Yes!

Those of us who start on this path know how effective it is for quieting the mind while silencing the internal noise and allowing a state of centredness and balance to flow. Today, most people experience overwhelm in everyday life, so knowing how to settle themselves through a meditative process is extremely beneficial.

I will do an abundance meditation once or twice a day for thirty days, and I can visually see the difference that ripples out in my life. The centredness and calmness is profound for emotional and mental well-being and overall healing.

I'm excited by the studies that show how parts of the brain get lit up through meditation, which is highly restorative.

How magnificent is it that the twenty minutes or so you give to yourself can be the switch for how much more dynamic your day is? Choosing to improve your life by including meditation and mindfulness will bring benefits of calmness and centredness.

We live in a fast-paced world. Even before this last pandemic hit in 2020, it was important to tune into the voice within, through stillness and quietness. It's a wonderful gift.

Why do you think people are working in a job they dislike?

I think people find it's easier to remain locked in and continue with the discomfort of what they know, versus taking the risk and making a change towards something they may like better.

The fear of failure is fed so constantly in our society through negativity and tall poppy syndrome, and it keeps people locked in. There's a focus on stories of what goes wrong, versus the examples of who's been successful and what's possible.

I do feel that if we don't change and evolve our mindset, it's easy to fall into doing the same old, same old, year in and year out. And most people do stay locked in, until either a traumatic event takes place or something that results in a deep emotional impact, causes the shift.

This impact gives them the jolt and a wakeup call, and ignites the desire to stop procrastinating and make a decision. It saddens me to see people settle, when they could really be pursuing what they're passionate about. Having personally stepped across this chasm, I understand how daunting it can be, and I understand why people choose not to go after what they want.

Chele Tindall

How can people become their own success story?

By setting a path for your life and not allowing external events to deviate you off-course. Clarify what success means to you. Don't just blindly follow the crowd.

I know that for me, when I was starting on my path, I didn't know my destination fully, but I took the first step anyway. When you learn to trust your internal GPS as you move forward, your certainty grows. Align yourself with a coach, don't look back and success will be yours.

To discover more about how Chele can help you *Elevate Your Results*, simply visit www.elevatebooks.com/results

Michelle Chan
The Inner Path to Success

Michelle Chan (陳綺婷) is an ICF Internationally Certified Coach and award-winning volunteer with a Human Resources background, who's passionate about helping people crystalise their definition of success. Having worked in several leading multinational corporations, she's assisted organisations in bringing out the very best in their employees at all levels.

Michelle is dedicated to helping people from all walks of life recognise their potential and shift their disempowering thoughts, so they can continue on their own journey of self-realisation. Through her extensive travels, volunteering and life experiences, she has the unique ability to meet people where they're at, gain an understanding of their world and help them find the perfect harmony between their personal and professional lives.

Michelle Chan

The Inner Path to Success

What is the biggest life lesson you have learned?

We're all on the rollercoaster ride of life, with its ups and downs, twists and turns. Who we choose to ride with, as well as our attitude, frames our experiences. The important thing to remember is that the journey isn't meant to be faced alone.

What I've learned is that in every single moment, there are lessons to be learned, wisdom to be extracted and something to be grateful for. But even so, the wisdom and lessons might not be immediately apparent and may only be discovered in hindsight upon deep reflection.

If you were speaking to your younger self, what advice would you give?

Time is the only constant. It's the levelling currency for everyone on earth. In this very moment, we're the youngest we will ever be. And even though we plan, we can't ever predict what happens next, so we owe it to ourselves to enjoy the micro-moments and make the most of them.

The advice I would give to my younger self, which are also the points I've come to live by, are the following:

- Be truly present in every moment. This is a simple idea, but in an ever-changing and fast-paced world, it's easy to get caught up in the busyness of life. For me personally, being present in the moment is a conscious practice.
- In everything you choose to accomplish, make sure you do it with your whole heart. It takes the same amount of time to perform

tasks half-heartedly as it does to get it done right, so always do your very best. While this is so, you also shouldn't let perfectionism creep in to stop you from completing the action or project. There are often timeframes and deadlines in place, so remember to also ensure you keep moving forward.

- Heraclitus, the Greek philosopher, had a view that "everything flows" and that "nothing endures but change". Be open to change, as it's going to happen. Take the opportunities that come your way, even when you don't feel quite ready (especially when you don't feel ready). Embrace them and make the most of them.

- Give yourself permission to courageously pursue your dreams and to shine. But while doing so, remember to practice self-care and maintain healthy boundaries. Continue to honour and respect yourself as much as you respect others.

- Your mindset and attitude are key. Having a positive, resilient mindset and attitude is a choice. It's a muscle that needs to be regularly exercised. Choose to view the world through a lens of gratitude and thankfulness. Choose to take actions that light you up, give you lasting joy and allow you to live a life of purpose and fulfilment.

- Always be kind to yourself and others, and remember that everyone is trying to do the best they can. We don't know their story, so don't be too quick to judge.

- Spend time with your loved ones and surround yourself with a community that lifts you up. Know that every person enters your life for a reason, a season or a lifetime, and that there are no coincidences in life. In addition to your health, the connections/relationships you have with a higher order/spirit/God, your loved ones and individuals you meet, are the most important aspects of your life. Everything else, such as possessions and money, can be replaced. So choose to spend quality time with your loved ones, and forgive quickly when it's required. The memories you create are priceless. No one can take them away from you.

Michelle Chan

Have you had any aha moments that changed everything for you?

There are many pivotal moments in my life that have shaped who I am today. Some are based on my own decisions and actions, while others have happened to me as a result of someone else's decisions and actions.

One key moment was my parents' choice to take the giant leap of faith and migrate from Hong Kong to Sydney, Australia in 1990. It was a decision that changed the course of my life. Had we not relocated, my life today would be very different. I'm infinitely grateful for the courage of my parents. They made the brave decision to relocate our family from a place where we were completely connected and supported, and step into the unknown.

We had to build a support network from scratch, learn a new set of customs and also overcome discrimination. Throughout my life, and especially during the period of settling into a new country, my parents showed my sister and me the true meaning of resilience and the importance of having faith. They were also role models for going into every situation with a sense of curiosity, rather than judgement, and to always meet people with kindness, even when the world was unkind. Some other important lessons we learned were:

- The importance of developing a sense of curiosity.
  It allows us to see the world through a lens of wonder.

- Always having a desire to learn something new.
  My parents highlighted the importance of applying ourselves to our studies and lessons learned beyond the traditional classroom. They taught us to be 'street smart' in addition to being 'book smart'. We learned to view every situation as a classroom, which gave us a chance to learn and to grow into better versions of ourselves.

- Meet people with kindness and curiosity.
  This enables us to be more empathetic and understanding towards others. It also helps eliminate prejudice, judgment and incorrect assumptions that can cause misunderstanding, miscommunication, friction and strained relationships.

- Too much of anything isn't good for you.
  The key is to achieve a sense of balance and to make sure you get enough rest. It's just like when you go to the gym. While it may feel like the effort/work is happening while you're exercising, it's actually during the rest periods/recovery stage that the muscle is being strengthened.

This also brings to mind another key moment in my life when I was suffering from a debilitating back issue. While at the time I felt like I was trapped with no way out, in retrospect, I can see it was a signal for me to pause and regroup my life.

The back issue was the last straw. I'd already been suffering from a severe case of burnout due to the accumulation of being overworked, coupled with the lack of balance, as well as poor posture. It had taken its toll on my body mentally and physically. Left unchecked, it eventually manifested itself in an unexpected and seemingly shocking way that impacted my quality of life. It was an important lesson for me to start listening to my body and honour whatever I was feeling, so I could ultimately respect myself. From that moment onwards, I made the conscious decision to continually take the necessary actions and give myself breaks in order to maintain balance in my life.

- Continue learning the lessons.
  After recovering from my back trouble, I came to realise the universe would constantly provide me with feedback, until I

learned the appropriate lessons, which in this case was pausing, listening to my body and providing it with the necessary rest and treatment.

When I was in the corporate world, no matter how much I loved working with my clients and helping individuals achieve their professional and personal goals, I found that too much time at work with insufficient breaks caused me to burn out. As a result, I came to appreciate the importance of focus and truly living in the present. For instance, if I was on a holiday, I would remain focused on taking a well-deserved break and not fall into the temptation of checking my work emails.

I also came to understand that having restorative breaks and spending quality time with loved ones helped me gain perspective and allowed my mind to reset, which ensured that I was more productive. It was important for me to not only focus on nurturing my physical well-being, but my mental health as well.

These two key moments in my life were pivotal in making me who I am today. They got me to realise what was truly important, helped shape me into more of my authentic self and also highlighted the significance of continually taking risks and stepping out of my comfort zone.

What are your tips for getting through a difficult time in life?

It's important to give ourselves permission to pause when going through a difficult time. It enables us to reflect and re-evaluate, thereby allowing us to gain perspective.

Another way to gain perspective is by reaching out to others. This is one of the key lessons I learned when suffering from my back issue. While our tendency is to only share our 'good' news and keep 'bad' news to ourselves, it's important to not face difficult times alone. We should keep ourselves open and honest with a trusted group during the low points in our life and share our struggles in a vulnerable way, while also being careful not to fall into a victim mentality.

Reaching out to others is a sign of strength, not weakness. It's an action that demonstrates a respect for ourselves. By leaning into our vulnerability, we also allow others to reach out their hand in support and/or provide the appropriate resources to help us. In my situation, by opening up to others and remaining positive, I was able to lean on the support of my family and friends, especially when I felt like there was no hope. I was also referred to a team of medical practitioners who were instrumental in my full recovery and thankfully without the need for surgery.

In short, it was a crucial moment for me to realise the power of having a positive and resilient mindset, that no man is an island and how important it was to have a supportive community around me. I also came to appreciate that in every situation, we have a choice. A choice to pause, a choice to not be a victim and a choice to reach out to others for support.

I recognise this is harder said than done, particularly in the moment when it feels like you're in a deep, dark hole with no way out and all solutions seem impossible. What I now know in retrospect is that there's always a way out and someone who's willing to help. However, you need to take the first brave step by being open and vulnerable, so they're aware of your situation.

What is the best way people can achieve a healthy work-life balance?

The way to achieve harmony between your personal and professional life, is to have a deep appreciation and understanding of your values. In addition, you'll need to build healthy boundaries, and have an unwavering commitment to withhold them, in order to continue honouring yourself. It's also about being fully present in each and every moment. Balance is about being able to harmonise the motif and find the rhythm and rhyme in the musical manuscript of life. It's not about fully stopping the music, although there may be times we need to slow it down or press pause.

When in pursuit of a healthy work-life balance, it's important to remember that no man is an island, and that as social beings, we should reach out to each other for support and assistance.

How do friends and family affect your life?

Family and friends have a big impact on my life. I'm incredibly blessed; I have family who are friends, and I'm lucky to have friends who are the family I choose. They are my safety net, my cheerleaders through every season of my life. For me, they're one of the few things that remain constant, and I know I can count on them for sound advice. They provide love and unconditional support through the peaks and troughs of the rollercoaster of life. But as with any relationship, there are ups and downs, and it requires constant work and clear communication to constantly strengthen the bond.

What do you think is your life purpose?

My life purpose is to make a huge difference in other people's lives.

From a young age, I recognised the immense difference that other people, from loved ones to complete strangers, had on my life, so I fully appreciate the ripple effect that occurs even from small acts of kindness. I would not be the same person without the generosity of others, and so this has been a key driver for me to continue leading a life of service. From my high school years, I've constantly been involved in volunteering for various charities and causes, including taking on leadership roles at the local Leo Club (part of Lions Clubs

International) for eight years. My diversity of volunteering experiences has enabled me to empathise with people of all ages, walks of life and backgrounds, and given me the opportunity to offer them a helping hand, even before they recognised they needed it. As a result, I'm able to touch many lives and use my light to help others shine their own light in the world.

More specifically, my mission is to help people find the necessary language to articulate their purpose in life with crystal-clear clarity. During my time working with young autistic children as an applied behavioural analyst (ABA) therapist, I came to discover that while others may see an autistic child's behaviour as aggressive and unproductive, my viewpoint was that they were simply misunderstood. A big part of the issue was that these children had not yet been exposed to or taught the language needed to express their wants and needs in a socially acceptable manner. As a result, other people were unable to interpret and understand their actions/behaviours.

With time, attention and effort, as well as through intensive therapy sessions and essential play, these children learned the important skills of communication, social interaction and self-help, vital to their development. These tools formed the essential keys to unlocking their ability to communicate in a socially acceptable way. They were able to flourish and rapidly grow to reach their potential. The ripple effects of working with these children were tremendous. As they learned these vital skills, their interactions with their loved ones dramatically improved, and the level of connection deepened. In fact, the dramatic changes that resulted from our therapy sessions translated into one of my clients overcoming the disorder altogether, where they were no longer classified as Classical Autism.

Through my volunteering experiences, and my work as an ABA therapist, I recognised that for some individuals who exhibit unproductive or destructive behaviours, it may be their way of desperately crying out for love and compassion. They might have never previously experienced kindness or love in their life, and so we help them acquire the language of kindness by extending it to them. By being blessed with our generosity, the hope is that they learn to demonstrate kindness and eventually pay it forward to others.

What would you like your legacy be?

At the end of my life, the legacy I would like to leave is simply the notion that I've shown kindness and made a difference in the lives of others. As one of Maya Angelou's quotes says, "I've learned that people will forget what you said, people will forget what you did, but people will never forget how you made them feel". I would like to be remembered for helping others feel supported, loved in their time of need and filled with a sense of belonging. As I grew older, I realised 'home' could be more than a physical place. It could also be a person, and the feelings of security, love and comfort that are associated with them.

When I think back to 2008, during my first trip visiting the place in rural China where my ancestors are from, I came to realise the legacy my grandmother left from gifting a simple rice cooker during one of her visits many years ago. It was my very first time meeting those family members, and my mother hadn't been back for many years.

No words can describe the warm welcome and love we experienced. What I found out was that even though a lot of the younger generations had not met my grandmother in person, as she passed away in 1999, there was a rice cooker she'd gifted their family many years back that continues to be remembered. Of course, it wasn't the rice cooker per se, but the feeling of care, comfort and security it gave to my ancestors during tough times. I have no doubt that my grandmother knew it would make a difference, but I don't think she could have envisaged the level of impact it still has, long after it's been discarded.

As human beings, we fall into the tendency of only taking action once everything is planned out, all the risks are assessed and we know exactly the results we seek to achieve. In reality, this level of perfectionism halts us and prevents us from living our lives. It's a reminder not to let the simplicity of the gesture, and the seemingly small impact we think it's going to have, stop us from taking the action. We should not underestimate the power of small gestures and gifts, as often the impact and ripple effect are more than we can ever imagine.

What mindset do you believe is needed to live a life of purpose and fulfilment?

The power of the mind should not be underestimated. Generally speaking, every experience is essentially neutral. It's how we interpret it, and the meaning we attribute to it, that determines how we react and respond, and whether we classify it as positive or negative. This can also be influenced by a variety of different factors, including our previous experiences, how society and/or we view it, and ultimately comes down to our mindset. But in the end, what we focus on and act upon, is determined by our values.

A game-changer moment for me was learning how to master my own shadow values, a concept termed by Benjamin J Harvey. Unlike golden values, which are the ones we show the world, such as service and compassion, we keep our shadow values hidden from the world. This would include such traits as control and superiority, even though they're arguably more powerful. When a person is triggered by a situation, it's about understanding which shadow values need to be appropriately fed to remain emotionally balanced. It's important to remember that the goal isn't to eliminate the negative, as that's impossible, but to learn to live in a balanced and harmonious manner and deal with whatever comes our way.

Mindset is a muscle that requires constant exercise. I have a simple daily practice of writing in my gratitude journal, which helps me maintain an attitude of gratitude. By living in this way, it enables me to go through my day with an open and curious mind and see each moment through the lens of thankfulness.

How can people become their own success story?

Success is a subjective term. Each person has their own unique definition of what it looks like to them, and the results they would like to achieve. Furthermore, as with every journey, someone's values may change depending on what's happening at the time. People can become their own success story by achieving the results they set out to accomplish through fully honouring their values and being empowered to pursue them with confidence.

Ultimately, it all starts with you.

You adopting and maintaining a positive mindset, having an unwavering belief you can achieve anything you want in life and possessing the courage and tenacity to pursue it. You do this by putting in the effort and surrounding yourself with people who will help get you to the next level.

What stops someone from achieving the success they really want?

There are several potential barriers that can stop someone from achieving their success story:

- If an individual doesn't fully understand and recognise their own values, they may stop themselves from initiating action, or the action they do take may not be in alignment with fulfilling what they truly desire.
- They may compare themselves to others. The danger of comparison is that it has the potential to rob people of their path to success.

While it can often be something they naturally fall into, and may fuel some to continue on their journey at a faster rate, it also may breed jealousy and self-doubt. It can then affect their mindset and hinder their ability to accomplish their desired results.

Remember to stay in your own lane, as the world has enough room for everyone to share their unique gifts and talents.

Do you have an approach to helping people achieve their success story?

My four-step framework, the 4Cs, will help you achieve your success story and live a life of purpose and fulfilment.

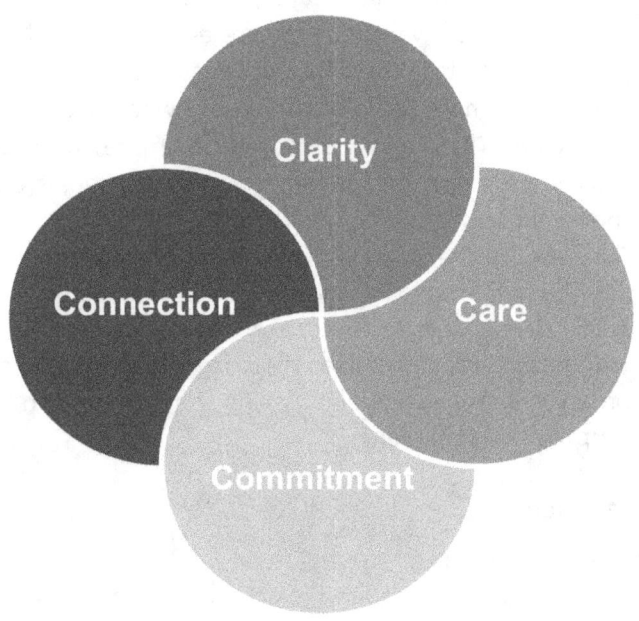

- **Clarity**

  - Be aware of what drives you, what truly matters to you and what and why you want to achieve in your life. Also, make sure you have crystal-clear clarity of your vision. All of this is essential to living a life of purpose and fulfilment.
  - Seek clarity, but remember that it isn't a one-stop shop, as we're constantly changing and evolving, so our values may transform over time.

- **Care**

  While having clarity is important, it's not enough. You also need to care.

  - Follow your heart. This means you not only need to be clear about what you want, but to care about the result. Build a plan, and then take the necessary actions to turn your dreams into reality. There's a visible difference when people do things with care. They're more motivated, more inspired, more passionate and more driven towards their goals and what they want to achieve.
  - Care about others and yourself. Demonstrate kindness often, and be generous. Establish healthy boundaries, maintain balance and practice self-care. Prioritising self-care helps you better tackle obstacles that may potentially hinder your progress and is essential in paving the way for living a life of purpose and fulfilment.

- **Commitment**

  With any action plan, there are several levels of effort and commitment that are required to achieve your success story.

  - Stay committed to your values and your plan. All too often, societal pressures and your inner critic can get in the way and deter you from making progress. Don't get side-tracked, and remember to remain laser focused.

- Be open to trial and error, and embrace any setbacks and failures as learning opportunities. While exciting, it can be daunting to dream big and to embark on something new. The path isn't always clear, so remember to be patient, and take the time to acquire the language and skills that are vital to embarking on your new adventure. Be persistent, remain committed to keep going, to keep putting in the effort and to keep taking the necessary actions to achieve your results.
- While you pursue your dreams, be sure to commit to regular self-improvement, so you can continually become a better version of yourself. This can be achieved through constant learning, in and out of the traditional classroom.
- Enjoy the journey, and don't focus solely on the destination. Remember that life is the ultimate travel adventure, so savour every moment.

- **Connection**
  - Build connections to create a sense of community. We're social beings, and the year 2020 has highlighted the fact that we can't live our lives alone. It's taught us that connections don't necessarily need to be made face to face. They can be built from afar with the use of technology. By connecting with others, we cultivate a support network, which is our very own cheerleading squad to push us further and to be better. Don't underestimate the importance of engaging and surrounding yourself with a supportive community, in order to live your success story and achieve a sense of fulfilment and purpose.
  - Live a life of service. The notion of connection and community is more than reaching out to others for support and building a network of cheerleaders. It's also appreciating that to truly live a life of fulfilment and purpose, we need to serve others to uncover our true authentic selves. In being of service, we're not only helping these people, but also providing ourselves

Michelle Chan

with an incredible opportunity to learn from each other and create a ripple effect where the benefits we see are only the tip of the iceberg.

To discover more about how Michelle can help you *Elevate Your Results*, simply visit www.elevatebooks.com/results

Markus O. Winzer
Leading through Being

Markus Ottomar Winzer is an effectiveness and results coach, international best-selling author and speaker, who's also an award-winning sales leader, with two decades of business experience in leading teams on three continents.

Continuously searching for ways to get to the next level in life, love and business, Markus taught himself how to push his limits to succeed. His goal has always been to discover what life would be like when you're the best version of yourself.

Markus combines his business experience and professional development to support CEOs, business owners and professionals to create high-performing teams, scale their businesses and find their next level of effectiveness, both in their business and personal life.

Markus O. Winzer

Leading through Being

What's the best thing that's ever happened to you, and why?

When I was eight years old, I was in the backseat of my parents' old car, filled with excitement and hope. We were on our way back from my grandmother's house, and I was watching the BMW and Mercedes cars zoom by, *whooom, whoom*, going 180 km/hr, while our car could only go about 80 km/hr.

I was filled with a mixture of admiration, joy and curiosity whenever we shared our highway with people from West Berlin. For some background, you should know that Berlin was divided by a wall from 1961 onwards, which was known as the Iron Curtain. It was like a separation of two realities. So if you lived in West Berlin and wanted to visit your family or friends in West Germany, you had to cross East Germany and were mandated to not divert from the highway.

You might say, "What's the big deal? Just cross one border, and that's it". Not this border. If you drove off the main highway or had any type of contact with an East German citizen, you could be detained, and the East German you contacted would be interrogated in a secret prison. Your lives would be at risk, with both of you in a place nobody could find you.

So with all of this in mind, why was I filled with excitement?

Well, I thought maybe today was the day we would stop at my favourite place, the petrol station. As an eight-year-old, for me it wasn't only a petrol station, it was access to happiness and joy, even if it was only for a few moments. I would walk into the transit shop and admire all of the remote-controlled Caterpillar trucks, toys and all the things we in East Germany couldn't buy, because they simply weren't available or allowed. In addition, even if we wanted to purchase a Coca Cola, a pair of Levi's or a Kinder Surprise, we didn't have the West German currency, which at the time traded at ten to one, or ten East German Marks for one West German Mark.

Have you ever been in the position of wanting something so bad but didn't have the means to get it in that moment? That one place represented my greatest fear and immense joy, because I would always think, *This time, I might get lucky...*

So my heart jumped with joy when my dad said, "Okay I will buy you an ice cream today!" It's such a vivid memory, I can recall exactly how it looked and tasted. The inside had vanilla with nuts, and it was covered in chocolate.

Two days later, we went through a hole in the Berlin Wall. A massive block had been broken out, and we lined up with everyone else. As we walked into a new world on the other side of Berlin, a beggar on the side of the road said to me, "Here, take these twenty West Deutschmarks, and buy yourself something nice to wear". We were overwhelmed by the generosity.

This was truly the best thing that happened to me. Now, at thirty-nine years old and looking back at my life, I understand this meant we were free to travel and give our opinion without fear of being thrown into jail. I was free to choose who I wanted to be.

Whenever I watch the movie *The Lives of Others* or read the book *Stasiland*, I pinch myself, because I'm grateful to be free and able to make the most of today. As Anna Funder characterises the GDR in *Stasiland*, "People were crazy with pain and secrets".

I could not have summarised it better than Bronnie Ware in her book *The Top 5 Regrets of the Dying*:

"Life doesn't owe us anything.
We only owe ourselves, to make the most of the life we are living,
of the time we have left, and to live in gratitude".

Today, I look with gratitude at my life and everything that has happened.

So what would your life look like,
if you would act from being grateful and free?
What would be possible for you and your teams?
What would happen to your business?

What is your biggest life lesson?

I visualised and dreamed of what it would be like to speak English, learn a new culture and visit this great nation that introduced me to Ronald Reagan, who said, "Mr. Gorbachev, tear down this wall!"

Two years later, I was in Medical Lake, a small community in Washington State, U.S.A., to play American football, basketball and tennis. I was learning English and had nightly homework in all six subjects, so I would study until five a.m. for the first three weeks. But my will to make it pulled me through. We call that *resilience*.

The lesson I received was that you can do anything if you put every ounce of energy into it and remain dedicated.

After coming back from the United States, I dreamed about what it would be like to collaborate with people from different nations. I asked myself, *What would it be like to work, lead and collaborate with no boundaries?* I closed my eyes and pictured myself fully engaged with a global team, the different cultures, personalities and approaches coming together to solve some of the world's most complex problems.

In 2010, I was working in Melbourne for six months, when I decided to follow my manager's request to fly to India and lead a large team. Next thing I knew, I was sitting in the back seat of a Jeep, driving through the streets of New Delhi. We were about to submit a proposal worth hundreds of millions of dollars for internet connectivity that would provide millions of Indians with access to knowledge, training and information online. After six weeks of leading more than thirty-five people from more than eleven different nationalities all around the world, we finally submitted the proposal.

One of the biggest lessons in my life so far has been learning how to follow my instincts and vision.

What is the worst thing that has ever happened to you, and how did you overcome it?

In 2017, my wife's former partner had just taken his life in Italy. He'd been depressed after having to close his business in Manly, Australia and go back home. We were in shock.

My first thoughts went to wondering if we could have done something about it. "What if" this and "what if" that.... There was just pain and hurt for someone who meant the world to my wife and was a friend to me.

So, the question became, "How can we become more aware, and what can we do?"

I found out that the Mental Health First Aid course equips healthy adults in recognising the signs and providing first-hand support for someone who may be unwell. We did the course, because we wanted the ability to identify the symptoms in family and friends.

So, my wife and I decided to create an initiative called Share2CareNow, to raise awareness about creating an environment that listens and supports people who might be struggling with their mental health. This is something everyone can do and is so empowering, as it can equip you with the skills to support someone in need.

What decisions have you made that changed your life?

Decision 1: Moving to the U.S.A. as an exchange student when I was seventeen.

I went to an American high school abroad in Medical Lake, a small community outside Spokane. I had to study and do a lot of homework in various subjects, all written in a language I barely spoke.

Looking back to that year, I realise how fortunate I was that my parents allowed me to go and supported me while I was there. Though my family helped me financially, I learned an important lesson about how to be self-sufficient. I realised I could survive anywhere in the world, no matter the location or circumstance. My persistence to stick with my tasks, as well as a deeply instilled confidence in myself and others, was built throughout the year.

Decision 2: Joining Siemens.

In 2002, after a year in the German Air Force and playing in a 7 nations tournament against the U.S.A., Great Britain, France and other countries, I decided to join the Management Accelerator Program with Siemens that enabled students to study, work and learn over four years. At the end, we received a full university degree, secondary qualification and two years' work experience. It gave me solid business acumen and first-hand experience in all areas of business, from procurement...to sales...to marketing...to management.

Decision 3: Becoming a sales and account manager.

In 2013, I made the decision to become a sales and account manager of a software business. In six years, we generated thirty-five-million dollars in revenue and contributed to one of the biggest infrastructure projects in Australia's history.

How are you currently making a difference in people's lives?

I use my twenty years of experience in leading large teams to create multiple million-dollar proposals that will empower business owners, managing directors and CEOs who want to take their business to the next level. I do this by utilising the methods, techniques and skills I've accumulated from my extensive business career, as well as what I've learned from training with Tony Robbins, Landmark, Ben Harvey, Engenesis creator Ashkan Tashvir and John Smallwood.

I work with my clients directly, one on one, as well as with their teams, to discover what's required at an end-to-end business level to unlock their full potential. From there, I'm able to help them create results, such as increasing their revenue and reducing costs, while maintaining their commitment to make a difference in the world.

What do you think people's biggest problems are?

Business owners, CEOs and managing directors, just like everyone else, can sometimes get stuck on how things appear to be. Maybe it's a failed business deal, where the customer simply doesn't make the purchase, that one employee who keeps forgetting to do the accounts or the business partner who hasn't delivered on the quality they promised. Here are some examples of how powerful people can doubt themselves:

- "Can I ask for what I want without people hating me?"
- "Have I hired the right team?"
- "Do I have the right processes, systems and tools?"

- "The team doesn't get it! I always wind up having to do it myself!"
- "I can't believe this is happening again!"
- "This isn't good enough. Is it because I'm not good enough, or they're not good enough?"

The dialogue has as much variety as humans on the planet. When we listen, argue or follow this internal chatter, our results will always remain limited to what we think, say or do. And if we achieve what we want, there will be a critical voice, so we compromise on peace of mind. This is where employees get fired or steal, customers get disappointed, mistakes happen and average results are achieved. The short and long-term consequences are that the business stays small, and business owners and managing directors burn out due to long hours and overnighters.

What's the best way to help them deal with this problem?

There are three simple steps that will help people move from stuck, stressed and overwhelmed, to being a powerful leader.

- **Step 1: Empower them to develop an awareness about what's blocking them from being a leader, so they can scale and improve their business.**
  Become interested in how you're being, rather than focussing on what you're doing. For instance, consider whether you're being
  - responsible
  - accountable
  - loving
  - contributing.

  Did you notice how Nelson Mandela interacted with his former prison guards? Was he resentful and blaming? No. He was loving, forgiving and ready to have the country move on to create a new joint future for South Africa. Undertaking a Being Profile®

Assessment will increase your awareness about how becoming an effective leader is the first step.

- **Step 2: Transform your way of being, so effective results show up.**
  I support leaders in transforming their way of being. For example, becoming confident in all areas of their business and taking one-hundred-percent ownership for all results.

- **Step 3: Get a coach.**
  I encourage you to get a coach for support. According to the International Coaching Federation (ICF), eighty-six percent of coaches report an increase in confidence under their guidance. A coach can support you in recognising how others see you and transform what's in the way of your breakthrough.

How does someone remain inspired?

It's important to keep being inspired, because it creates a feeling or mood that lets us achieve extraordinary results.

So how do you do it? Through habits or regular practices, you'll be able to install a rhythm and structures that will enable you to reflect, review and raise your awareness on a daily basis, as to what and why things are important to you.

Inspiration usually shows up when you're aware of what you want, why you want it and where you really want to go. So here are eight key steps to staying inspired:

1. Actively define what's important to you, and write it in a journal/book.
2. Clarify why it's important to you.

3. Communicate these to your family, your teams, your friends, your co-workers and your peers, and actively seek their opinion.
4. Make sure you allow yourself enough space to let your mind wander. Go on a ten-fifteen minute walk, or just sit outside in nature.
5. Enable an accountability buddy, someone who holds you accountable for the actions and results you're creating and who will check in with you on a daily/weekly basis.
6. Explore *habitshareapp.com* to track all of your habits/routines and enable your accountability buddy to support you on your journey.
7. Become interested in what inspires other people and what that inspiration means for you.
8. Put reminders all around that help you remain inspired. You can hang a picture on your mirror in the bathroom or put pictures/quotes up near your screen or laptop of people you admire.

Why are goals important?

Based on scientific evidence from psychology professor Dr. Gail Matthews, performance is influenced by three key actions: writing goals, committing to goal-directed actions and creating accountability for those actions. Seventy-five percent of all groups that performed all three key actions, reached their results, or at least got halfway there, versus the forty-three percent who neglected to complete at least one of them.

Write down your goals, and create accountability. But remember that goals by themselves aren't effective. It's only when you combine them with intention and action, in alignment with your plan, that you make progress.

You might also want to consider how you're being when taking action and creating your goals. Being responsible, accountable and having confidence will enable you to take more effective action, communicate powerfully and make relevant requests.

How can someone find their life purpose?

Based on my life experience as a husband, son, citizen of the world and someone who's travelled and lived in more than three continents, I think I'm qualified to say that there are multiple ways to identify your life purpose.

In Victor E. Frankl's *Man's Search for Meaning*, he states that, "Everyone has his own specific vocation or mission in life; everyone must carry out a concrete assignment that demands fulfillment. Therein he cannot be replaced, nor can his life be repeated. Thus, everyone's task is unique, as is his specific opportunity to implement it".

For me, purpose is bigger than my own concerns for myself. It's a calling, a request and a drive.

Based on my own qualitative research, where I asked a selection of people about their purpose, how they defined happiness and what and why they took the actions they did, I recommend the following five steps to help you find your life purpose:

1. Set a time period for figuring it out. It could take a day, a week, a month or a year, but set a date as to when you can definitively say what your life purpose is.
2. Purchase a notebook, and thirty minutes prior to sleeping, write down any activities during the day that gave you the biggest sense of fulfilment and achievement.
3. Figure out in which areas you get the most fun, excitement and enjoyment.

4. Discover what you're naturally drawn to, what you want to create in this world and how you want to leave it.
5. Allow yourself to travel, explore and test your skills. Say yes to a new skill every day or month, so you can continue to grow.

What is your most inspiring client story?

Kristina, the business owner of a yoga studio here in Sydney, was able to increase her profits by twenty percent within six weeks of starting my coaching program. We discovered in the Being Profile® Assessment report which way of being would make the biggest shift and impact in her business. She transformed her confidence, forgiveness and assertiveness, and became bold with her requests to customers, staff and partners.

One of my clients who was anxious all the time and felt unfulfilled, realised she had the power to create the life she wanted. She discovered that there was nothing wrong with her and that she'd been stuck in her stories of "I'm not good enough" and "I can't do this". She learned how to be present regarding her possibilities and now feels she's truly living her life. She's taking on more responsibilities at work and accepting new, more high-profile assignments. She realised that to be successful in her professional life, a wholistic approach was needed regarding her career and other parts of her life.

There was a client who had three choices regarding how to adjust his business, so it could thrive after the negative impact COVID-19 had on the company. He felt stuck and didn't know which path he should choose to move forward.

Undertaking the Being Profile® Assessment, and working with me, helped him achieve clarity. He absolutely loved the highly analytical, systematic approach to disentangling the many thoughts about his choices, so he could come to a clear conclusion as to which option would make the most sense, both from a business and a personal perspective.

He was able to choose a path without any further inhibitions, and the business took off completely within a matter of not even two weeks after the coaching sessions. I helped him find his inner compass in these often-confusing times, which allowed him to sail his boat into waters where the wind blew the strongest.

Another client had a financial blockage and wanted to identify ways he could increase his confidence and get unstuck in the area of finance. During our coaching sessions, he discovered what was stopping him and got the clarity he needed. He now feels a lot more confident and financially abundant.

What courses have you taken that enabled you to get started or build your business?

Over my lifetime, I've invested more than 100,000 Australian dollars into my own education. I've also devoted many years to sales training and more than five different transformation programs, including the Engenesis Thrive Coaching training, Tony Robbins Platinum Partnership, Ben Harvey/Authentic Education's PHD program, Hypnotherapy, NLP, and Landmark's programs, including the Team, Management and Leadership program. I've also received a Bachelor of Business Administration and had hundreds of trainings in business, management and leadership.

Do you have a coach, mentor or someone who motivates you?

I have been, and continue to be, mentored by Tony Robbins, Ben Harvey and Dean Graziosi. Here in Australia, I'm mentored by Ashkan Tashvir, the founder of Engenesis, and John Smallwood, who runs the Engenesis Thrive Coaching Program. I have coaches in several areas that include fitness, wealth, health and ontology. I believe that for us to be effective and accomplish what we want, we need to transform what stops us, and one of the most efficient ways is to have a coach.

How can people become their own success story?

There are several ways people can become their own success story. A key ingredient is self-awareness. A lot of times we look for more information, more steps, more tools and more tips and tricks. But we can't transform what we cannot see. The first and most basic step is to discover what we don't know we don't know.

You can increase your awareness with tools like the Being Profile®, the world's first ontological assessment tool, which was designed by Engenesis. It empowers you to increase your awareness, identify your way of being and your relationships, including key distinctions, such as responsibility, vulnerability and authenticity and many other ways of being, that are required to master becoming an effective leader. There are more than thirty ways of being that contribute to your success, and I bet you want to know what they are…

What is the one message you wish to share with the world?

I don't know about you, but I've always found it interesting that we're quick to write down our lists of actions we need to DO every day, month and year, all consisting of maybe a five or ten-year plan. And if we move forward, we think we're making progress.

At the same time, that list never runs out of actions and gets longer and longer during the day. Maybe the challenge isn't in the doing, but being effective with our actions and way of being. What if there's a choice, moment by moment, where I can choose to be a certain way? For example, I choose to be responsible, generous, loving and forgiving.

Margaret Heffernan, in her book *Wilful Blindness*, says that "As long as it (an issue) remains invisible, it is guaranteed to remain insoluble". Until you become interested in what story, belief, value and mindset influences you, then you won't become aware of or alter your outcomes, and would only be able to marginally influence the results in your life.

As a son, entrepreneur, managing director, business owner and member of our country and society, I'm interested in how the world is and not just my perception of it. I want to know how I'm being with myself and anyone around me.

My one message for everyone is to have them ask themselves these questions:
"How am I being, and is it effective?"
"How can I increase my awareness of how I'm being?"

 To discover more about how Markus can help you *Elevate Your Results*, simply visit www.elevatebooks.com/results

Afterword

While you were reading these people's inspiring stories, did you notice something? All of their life experiences were for a purpose, bringing them closer to their goals, relationships and especially the message they were meant to share with the world.

The last page is a blank canvas for you to write the next chapter of your own story about elevating your results and inspiring others. Every day is a brand-new opportunity to be the author of your destiny.

Next Steps

To support you on your journey to *Elevate Your Results,* we recommend you take advantage of these resources:

🖥 7 Day Transformation Program

Learn ONE powerful 'Elevate Process' you can use immediately to improve Your Relationships, Health, Finances, Mindset and any other area of your life.

To join this 7-day transformation online program, simply go to: www.elevatebooks.com/you

👥 Connect with the Authors

To discover more about the authors and what they have to teach you, and bonus gifts they are offering visit:
www.elevatebooks.com/results

🎤 Subscribe to our Podcast

If you'd like to hear the go-to interviews from the authors and be re-inspired, check out: www.elevatebooks.com/podcast

🌐 Visit the Website

To find out more about the Elevate book series, visit: www.elevatebooks.com

www.ingramcontent.com/pod-product-compliance
Lightning Source LLC
Chambersburg PA
CBHW071603080526
44588CB00010B/1001